CRYSTALS
for
PSYCHIC
SELF-PROTECTION

Books by Judy Hall

Non-fiction

Psychic Development, Flying Horse Press, 2014

Earth Blessings, Watkins Books, 2014

The Crystal Wisdom Oracle, Watkins Books, 2013

Crystals and Sacred Sites, Fair Winds Press, 2012

The Encyclopedia of Crystals (Revised), Godsfield Press and Fair Winds Press, 2012

The Crystal Bible, Volumes I, II and III, Godsfield Press, 2003, 2009 and 2012

101 Power Crystals, Fair Winds Press, 2011

Life Changing Crystals, Godsfield Press, 2011

The Book of Why, Flying Horse Press, 2010

The Soulmate Myth, Flying Horse Press, 2010

Crystal Experience, Godsfield Press, 2010

Good Vibrations, Flying Horse Press, 2008

Crystal Love, Godsfield Press, 2007

Crystal Prescriptions Volumes I and II, O Books, 2005

Crystal Healing, Godsfield Press, 2005

The Astrology Bible, Godsfield Press, 2005

The Crystal Zodiac, Godsfield Press, 2004

Fiction

Torn Clouds, O Books, 2005

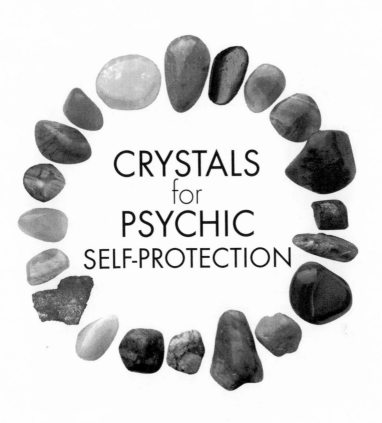

CRYSTALS
for
PSYCHIC
SELF-PROTECTION

JUDY HALL

HAY HOUSE

Carlsbad, California • New York City • London • Sydney
Johannesburg • Vancouver • Hong Kong • New Delhi

First published and distributed in the United Kingdom by:
Hay House UK Ltd, Astley House, 33 Notting Hill Gate, London W11 3JQ
Tel: +44 (0)20 3675 2450; Fax: +44 (0)20 3675 2451; www.hayhouse.co.uk

Published and distributed in the United States of America by:
Hay House Inc., PO Box 5100, Carlsbad, CA 92018-5100
Tel: (1) 760 431 7695 or (800) 654 5126
Fax: (1) 760 431 6948 or (800) 650 5115; www.hayhouse.com

Published and distributed in Australia by:
Hay House Australia Ltd, 18/36 Ralph St, Alexandria NSW 2015
Tel: (61) 2 9669 4299; Fax: (61) 2 9669 4144; www.hayhouse.com.au

Published and distributed in the Republic of South Africa by:
Hay House SA (Pty) Ltd, PO Box 990, Witkoppen 2068
Tel/Fax: (27) 11 467 8904; www.hayhouse.co.za

Published and distributed in India by:
Hay House Publishers India, Muskaan Complex, Plot No.3, B-2, Vasant Kunj, New Delhi 110
070; Tel: (91) 11 4176 1620; Fax: (91) 11 4176 1630; www.hayhouse.co.in

Distributed in Canada by:
Raincoast Books, 2440 Viking Way, Richmond, BC V6V 1N2
Tel: (1) 604 448 7100; Fax: (1) 604 270 7161; www.raincoast.com

A catalogue record for this book is available from the British Library.

ISBN 978-1-78180-384-4

To the memory of Christine Hartley, without whose wisdom I would know little, and to my clients and workshop participants, without whom I would know even less, and to all those who, by their actions and reactions, ensured I would learn rather more than I wished to know. My gratitude and blessings to you all.

Contents

Preface: *Learning by Experience*   ix
Introduction: *Feeling Safe in an Uncertain World*   xv

Part I: Protection Tools

Self-Protection Tools   5
  Tool 1: Your Crystal Treasure Chest   6
  Tool 2: Crystal Layouts   14
  Tool 3: Amulets   15
  Tool 4: Relaxation Crystals   17
  Tool 5: Gem Essences   18
  Tool 6: Journalling   19
  Tool 7: The Bubble of Light   20
  Tool 8: The Golden Pyramid   23
  Tool 9: Breathing   25
  Tool 10: Getting Grounded   28
  Tool 11: Intention and Focus   30
  Tool 12: Trust   34
  Tool 13: Affirmations   36
  Tool 14: Visioning and Re-visioning   37
  Tool 15: Ceremony   40
  Tool 16: Positive Thought   42
  Tool 17: Guardian Angels   44
  Tool 18: Psychic Shields   47
  Tool 19: Vision Boards   49
  Tool 20: Traditional Symbols   49
  Tool 21: Journeying   53
  Tool 22: Smudging   55
  Tool 23: Gratitude and Blessing   56
  Tool 24: Believing in Yourself   58

Tool 25: Happiness   59
Tool 26: Animal Allies   61
Tool 27: Crystal EFT   65

Part II: Eliminate the Negative

Creating Safe Spaces   71
Healthy Boundaries   97
Your Psychic Immune System   105
Foiling the Energy Pirates   117
Detoxification   127
Transmuting Toxic Emotions   147
Reversing Mental Overload   162
Neutralizing the Attackers, Whoever They Are   176
Protecting Family and Friends   199

Part III: Accentuate the Positive

Finding Inner Peace   206
Finding Serenity   209
Enhancing your Spiritual Equilibrium   217
Opening the Higher Chakras   223
Finding Abundance   236
Feeding your Body and Soul   243
Holding the Vision   246

Afterword   251
Notes and References   253
Resources   255
Further Reading   257
Index   259

Preface

LEARNING BY EXPERIENCE

'This book is not, and cannot be, a satisfactory handbook
for the treatment of psychic disorders. All it can do is to
point in the directions where enquiries might be pursued
with advantage. If it serves to direct attention to certain
subjects that badly need investigation it will have fulfilled
its purpose.'

Dion Fortune, *Psychic Self-Defense*[1]

In the conclusion to what is probably the best-known
psychic protection book of all time, *Psychic Self-Defence*,
written in 1930, Dion Fortune threw down the challenge
that others should take her work further. For over 45
years, ever since I had the pleasure of meeting Christine
Hartley, her literary agent and metaphysical colleague, I've
taken up that challenge, not through choice but through
necessity. Like Dion herself, I had to learn psychic protection
techniques 'on the hoof' when I came under severe psychic
attack. But unlike her I was not involved in magical working.
My experience was more prosaic: people I'd inadvertently
upset in my everyday life attacked using their personal
malevolent will and the power of thought, although one

at least did have occult knowledge to call on. In addition, I realized how important everyday self-protection was as I became increasingly aware of my sensitivity to auras, energies and environments – and of the workings of my own inner psyche, which was not above carrying out a psychic mugging or two of its own, often on me.

- **Psychic attack:** Concentrated and conscious malevolent thought and intent directed towards someone to bring about harm.
- **Psychic mugging:** Being hit by a blast of negative energy.
- **Aura:** The subtle biomagnetic sheath that surrounds the physical body.

Fortunately, for several years I had the unfailingly wise counsel of Christine to call on and she shared many techniques with me, some of which form the basis for this book, although I've expanded them to adapt to changing situations and my deeper understanding of what may lie behind apparent psychic attack and noxious energy situations. My own studies into crystals, metaphysics and psychology have furnished further avenues for exploration and many more insights into how we can be our own inner terrorist, as has working with what must by now be thousands of people in workshops and 'far memory' karmic readings that look at the deeply ingrained patterns and expectations we have brought into this present life from our previous lives (an area which can leave us vulnerable but which I've chosen not to address in this book as I've covered it elsewhere[2]).

I've written several books on psychic protection, each one building on the last and each arising out of a major change or challenge in my own life and further insights into why protection is needed. So why, you might ask, did I choose to write yet another one, and then update it? Well, this time the book is in response to world changes that affect everyone and looks at things from a slightly different perspective. It's particularly angled towards people who have never before thought they might need self-protection but who are finding the world an increasingly challenging place or who are caught up in the rapid expansion of consciousness sweeping over our world. Fortunately crystals and other tools give us a way to protect ourselves easily and safely, and more of them are now available.

The book is also intended for anyone who is following the psychic, spiritual or magical path. The success of 'celebrity psychics' on the entertainment scene in the UK, the proliferation of psychic phone lines and the creation of dedicated TV channels are opening up the metaphysical world to everyone and it is now more accessible than ever before. But this brings its own pitfalls. Once, in the esoteric world, access to the worlds beyond this one had to be earned by careful study and long practice. Initiation was followed by closely supervised experience. Nowadays, anyone can pick up a book and learn how to be psychic in five minutes – but they are rarely taught how to close the ability down again. Dion Fortune's advice, Christine Hartley's edict and my own credo have always been: 'Don't meddle. Do only what you are trained to do.'

When I started teaching psychic self-protection, it was to youngsters who had been playing with a ouija board and were in danger of being overwhelmed by mischievous spirits or the odd poltergeist, and there was always a need to move on spirits who hadn't quite cottoned on to the fact they had passed over to another world. Nowadays it is more likely to be 'alien beings' trying to take over the world who are, allegedly, causing trouble, or so-called higher beings that are anything but. But people attracted by the excitement and glamour of the spirit world – and it's wise to remember that in the old days glamour meant 'spell' rather than appearance – are also in need of self-protection, especially from their own selves, as we will see.

> • **Psychic self-protection:** Creating a safe space around and within yourself, screening out unwanted thoughts, feelings and energies from, and preventing energy loss to, other people or the environment.

There are many of us who believe the Earth is undergoing great changes at this time. Shifts of consciousness, a raising of vibrations, an influx of new energies – call it what you will. As an astrologer, I call it the transition to the Age of Aquarius. Others call it the ascension process, but some see it as the potential ending of the world. They speak of great traumas and dramas, natural disasters overwhelming the Earth. That's their reality. Mine is different. I believe we'll get the kind of world we create with our thoughts and actions now. If we make a shift in our thinking and begin to treat the Earth as sacred once more and all the beings – human or otherwise – on the planet as our brothers and sisters, and if we raise our own vibrations, we have an opportunity for positive change. I believe we can all live intuitively and creatively from an open heart and I'd like to invite you to join me in that worldview.

I hope anyone who is facing the challenge of change or who is widening their perception and raising their level of consciousness, from the novice to the most experienced metaphysical practitioner, will find this book helpful, so that we all can, in the words of Margaret Koolman, 'relax into what's going on without being defended and afraid'. Knowledge is, after all, one of the most potent forms of protection there is.

Judy Hall

Treasure Chest

LABRADORITE

The number one protection crystal, Labradorite creates an interface around you that filters out energies that are not to your benefit and enhances your spiritual connection. It allows you to be aware of other people's feelings and energies without being overwhelmed by them. Enhancing your psychic abilities, it aligns the physical and subtle bodies and strengthens the aura.

Introduction

FEELING SAFE IN AN UNCERTAIN WORLD

'It is not the strong that survive, nor the most intelligent. It is those with the ability to adapt to change.'
Charles Darwin

In this rapidly changing and stressed-out world, we're all looking for security and certainty, and there is one thing that gives you an unshakeable feeling of safety. That is a sense of inner peace, of being at home and, therefore, protected in your own skin. Once you have that, no matter what happens around you, you're ready to meet challenges with excited anticipation and the confidence of being in charge of your own destiny. Rather than taking a defensive stance, you open yourself up and meet the world with joy and optimism. And, as what you focus your attention on manifests, your world becomes better and better as you adapt to change. Fortunately there are some wonderful tools available to support that feeling of inner peace, the foremost being crystals.

There is an enormous difference between psychic self-protection that creates inner safety and the fear-based defences that lock you up behind a wall, and you'll probably be surprised what your mindset can do. We create and attract to ourselves what we fear most, but we can equally well attract positive and beneficial vibes if we put our mind to it. A positive attitude quickly overcomes a negative one and creates a natural feeling of safety. Once you have this, once you no longer worry or fear, you naturally trust the universe around you – and yourself. If you feel safe inside, the outer world won't appear threatening – challenging maybe, but in a good way. It's simply a question of changing how you view things.

As you will discover, the things that tend to trip us up are the expectations we have, the toxic emotions we hold on to, the ingrained belief patterns and obsessive thoughts that go round and round in our head and the language we use to express what is going on in our life. Change those, and make a deeper connection to our spiritual self, and we change our life.

What also trips us up is getting caught up in the glamour of contact with the 'spirit world' and the excitement of spells and incantations. Chanting for wealth and asking the cosmos to provide, for instance, have their own pitfalls, but common sense, discretion and a few pointers to sensible working in the relevant field soon overcome these.

This book contains numerous tools to help you help yourself, but the greatest is one you already possess: the power of your own mind. If you look positively at the world, you have natural self-protection. Being able to laugh at yourself and at the idiosyncrasies of all worlds is also an excellent deterrent. Little that's toxic survives the benevolent glow of good humour.

There are many simple – and effective – ways to enhance your energy level and boost self-protection that have been used for thousands of years, which include crystals, but the focus has to be on taking charge of your own thoughts and feelings. When you trust and believe you're safe and power-full, you are.

But isn't there a paradox here? Yes, there is, because what is being suggested is that if you feel safe you won't need self-protection and yet this book is giving you protection tools. This may seem contradictory, but there are good reasons for it. I know, for instance, that it's possible that you may unknowingly harbour a terrorist in your inner self, or you may be on the receiving end of a psychic mugging, or live in an area of geopathic stress, or suffer from electromagnetic stress, and so need to take remedial measures. I know some people experience serious psychic attack that devastates their well-being, but I also know a sense of proportion is essential if you are not to overreact and exacerbate a situation.

> • **Geopathic stress:** Stress created by electromagnetic radiation, ley lines, underground water and such like. It's also present in 'sick building syndrome'. Injurious to health, it can affect the immune system as well as the body's innate psychic protection and may attract 'ghosts' or hold impressions of previous events.
>
> • **Electromagnetic stress:** Disharmony caused by the subtle emanations of electrical, microwave, computer, phone and radio frequencies and power lines.

I'm aware there is what might be deemed paranoia in some quarters about alien or evil entities bent on destroying us, and it's easy to get caught up in this – although an old meaning of 'paranoia' is 'knowledge at the edge of awareness', so a judicious application of common sense is needed, together with discrimination about what you read and where you put your attention. There's an enormous amount of doom and gloom being put out in the media, together with a great deal of psychic drivel. I also know that if you put too much of your attention on thinking about protection, constantly worrying about it, you draw to yourself that which you fear, and yet there may also be times when you inadvertently walk into something energetically noxious or unexpectedly trigger someone's wrath or envy, and then it's a little late to be learning self-protection methods.

So how do you resolve this? Well, you practise protection techniques in a spirit of fun, with a 'let's try this and see how it makes me feel' kind of approach, and you trust that you're protected and so don't need to worry. You also pay attention to your subconscious self, hoicking out any mental programmes or toxic emotions that are undermining you. Crystals can help you to do this, and these and the other easy-to-use techniques given here can be applied to all areas of your life. Then, if you do need protection, it comes into play automatically.

• **Crystal:** All-embracing term for a gem, precious or semi-precious stone, mineral ore, resin or fossil.

So What Exactly Is Psychic Self-Protection?

Perhaps we should first look at what it's not, in order to dispel some common illusions around the word 'psychic'. It's not weird, flaky, new-agey – or godless and superstitious. And it doesn't mean checking your common sense into cold storage for the duration. Psychic gifts don't belong to the devil, no matter what you might have been told. They're an innate part of humanity's toolbox for dealing with change and understanding the world. 'Psychic' means 'belonging to the psyche': the fusion of mind, soul and spirit at the heart of a human being. But being psychic is also about being aware of subtle levels of reality, the (usually) unseen energetic dimensions that surround and interpenetrate with the physical. In other words, using your intuition.

Psychic self-protection is not about fighting anything off or battling with evil forces or any other such nonsense. It doesn't need spells and it certainly doesn't involve black magic or witchcraft. While it's dynamic in its effect and uses the power of intent, it's not threatening, and it's most definitely not about hurting anyone else or being aggressive towards those who don't have your best interests at heart. Self-protection is about feeling secure within your own self.

Psychic self-protection is about creating a safe space in which to live, work and have your being. It creates healthy boundaries and a calm, quiet centre in which to simply *be.* It's about having positive emotions and constructive thoughts that create a benevolent world. It isn't really about *doing*, it's all about creating through allowing. Psychic self-protection creates a tranquil space in which others cannot disturb your equilibrium – either deliberately or by what they think or feel spilling out into the atmosphere around them, an atmosphere to which you are inevitably sensitive to some degree. Body language, stance and facial expression and other subtle clues can alert you to how someone is feeling, but a part of your energy field, your intuition, will have already picked this up and given you signals in your own body. The trick is to be aware that it's done so but not to be overwhelmed by it. You can then choose to respond constructively. It's the same with places – we have all felt those chills down the spine or that headache that develops almost instantly in a particular place. If we recognize these feelings as signals that all is not well energetically, we can quickly take steps to transform the energy and to protect ourselves if necessary.

If you feel you're too open to other people's energies and vulnerable to psychic invasion, you can quickly close off with a traditional body posture that creates an energy circuit around your body that cannot be breached by outside influences:

Try This

When travelling on crowded public transport or sitting with a needy friend or at work, cross your arms over your solar plexus and cross your legs at the ankles to create an energy circuit that cannot be breached.

A time-honoured, constant and reliable means of protecting yourself is by wearing a crystal or keeping one in your pocket – although if you don't ask the crystal to work with you and keep it energetically clean afterwards, it can end up doing the opposite of what you intended it to do, so do remember to cleanse all your crystals regularly. Labradorite is particularly good for protecting your energies (*see pages xiii and 8*).

Why Crystals?

The ability of crystals to harness the power of your mind and enhance the tools given throughout this book is truly incredible. They amp up the energy and boost whatever you do, and they have a unique ability to absorb negative energy, which is why the self-protection tools in the book have 'treasure chests' of specific crystals and 'crystal tips' to lead you to other useful stones. A choice of stones is given because you might well already have a suitable crystal at home and because certain stones are suitable for particular people and other stones are more suited to someone else – not all people resonate at the same frequency or have the same sensitivity. Do remember, though, that crystals pick up the vibrations of everyone who handles them and is in their vicinity. This is why they need regular cleansing.

Crystals have been used for thousands of years to protect and enhance personal energy and to instil the qualities, such as confidence, that help you to feel safe in an uncertain world. Recipes for crystal protection have been found that are over 5,000 years old and the same crystals are still being used today. Bloodstone, Hematite and Carnelian, for instance, were placed around the wrists of newborn babies in Mesopotamia and Egypt to ensure a long, prosperous and safe life, and the same combination is still effective in modern times. In the Neolithic period – 'the Stone Age' – stones literally were the modern technology of the time. There is evidence from graves over 40,000 years old that crystals were used to protect the dead on their journey to the next world and we can assume that they were also used to protect the living. This tradition passed into Greece, Arabia, India and the Far East. This means such crystals are imbued not only with their own inherent properties but also the power of intent, expectation and long tradition.

So, you might well be asking, what inherent power does a crystal have? The honest answer to this is no one fully knows – yet. Although crystals may look solid, like everything else in the universe they are a seething mass of the orderly vibration of a few particles and a lot of space and, as the ancients would have argued, that space is filled with consciousness. The ancients believed that crystals, as with everything else on and in the Earth, were alive and, therefore, had sentient awareness. They were said to live on a different timescale from humans, taking a breath every hundred years or so. Many indigenous peoples believed they were the brain cells of Mother Earth.

Quantum physics, which comes closest to understanding the interaction of matter and consciousness, may eventually supply the full answer to how crystals work, but in the meantime we can definitely talk about their ability to focus energy – which is why they are used for lasers and computer chips – and the effect of vibration and colour. Colour is essentially a vibration of light and the human body is innately responsive to it. We also know that many crystals are piezoelectric – that is, they generate minute electrical currents that interact with the currents in the human body or the environment. Some contain traces of therapeutic minerals that pass through the skin barrier to bring about physiological changes. Kunzite, for instance, contains lithium, which is used by doctors to medicate depression and bipolar disorders. Crystal enthusiasts simply hold Kunzite or place it on their heart and feel uplifted. Other crystals, particularly black crystals such as Tourmaline or Smoky Quartz, have an internal lattice that traps energy within it. This means they soak up negative energy, but crystals also make the perfect receptacle for – and reminder of – your positive intention.

Further on in this book you'll find the basic information you'll need about choosing and caring for your crystals, together with tips on the crystals that are suitable for specific exercises and tasks. If you need further information, you'll find all you need to know about the specific properties of crystals in my books *The Crystal Bible Volumes I, II and III, 101 Power Crystals* and *Crystal Prescriptions Volumes I and II*.

Why Might You Need Protection?

There are many ways in which your natural self-protection can be undermined by both yourself and other people. Every time you say something negative, feel a lack or have a detrimental expectation, you weaken yourself. Every time you allow someone to draw on your energy, you become unhealthily vulnerable, as you do when you upset someone or attract their envy. And, without a doubt, there are some decidedly negative energies simply hanging about. A participant on one of my astrology retreats came back from a visit to Glastonbury town looking decidedly wobbly.

'I've been psychically mugged,' he said.

Glastonbury, like many spiritual centres, attracts a hotch-potch of people, from the highest to the most negative, few of whom are in charge of their own unsavoury energies. Many are spaced out and wide open to invasion and leak their energy wherever they go. The town has a strong drug culture and black as well as white magic is practised on top of ancient earth energy and spiritual sites: a recipe for psychic disaster.

This guy had unwittingly walked straight into a patch of extremely nasty energy which had hit him in the heart. He literally felt as though he'd had a heart attack – and this despite my having emphasized to those on the retreat that, having opened up higher levels of consciousness and their chakras, they needed to be meticulous in closing down and protecting themselves before they went into town. This was his first retreat and he'd only just got into spiritual work, having had his healing capacity open up rapidly. So, while he thought he was coming to learn about astrology, clearly he was also on an accelerated learning experience concerning self-protection and energy cleansing – essential for every healer. I also discovered later that he thought a safe distance for his aura was several feet out from his body – not a good idea in any crowded place, as we will see.

It was a useful object lesson for me, too. One of the first tasks for me when starting a retreat is to create an energetically safe space for the group and I'd put a grid of protection over the gateway to the house and all around the grounds, but he had been able to walk through it with the energy still attached. It showed that if someone who belongs in a safe space comes into it with something nasty attached, safe space alone isn't enough. After that,

I also deliberately placed a crystal filter to catch anything negative at the gates.

> • **Safe space:** A place, large or small, which is protected and cleansed so that nothing negative or untoward can penetrate or interfere with what goes on in that space.

Fortunately, 15 minutes with a piece of Tugtupite on his heart drew out the shaft of energy, dissolved the psychic pain and restored his well-being (*see page 177*). In the meantime, I was able to use crystals to dissipate the energy rather than sending it back out into Glastonbury where it could do more harm.

Other forms of 'psychic mugging' are more subtle. You've only to realize how the media relish inflating 'problems' to see that if you listen to the news or read a newspaper, you can be infected by doom and gloom, just like getting a nasty dose of 'flu standing in the checkout queue at the supermarket (*put yourself in the bubble of light on page 20; it works wonders*). It's an extreme example, but I had a friend with bipolar disorder who obsessively watched the coverage of the first Gulf War, which sent him over the edge into paranoid illusions and delusions from which he never really recovered. If you bombard yourself with those kinds of images and naïvely believe all you're told without questioning it, at the very least you will worry and fear – and these are two of the greatest underminers of security there are. But your own mind can create enough doomful scenarios to end the world by itself if you indulge in pessimistic thinking or allow negative emotions or thought patterns to prevail.

There's also the possibility of getting caught up in the huge psychic excitement that's being generated at the moment. I was asked to write a book called **Revelations of a Psychic**. The brief was to be as sensational as possible because, so I was told, this was what the mass market wanted. I refused, because I know that kind of thing draws prurient curiosity – and even animosity – from many levels, including the envious living and the unquiet dead. If you are going to engage with the over-sensationalized psychic world, it's best to have some protection tools at the ready first. I've seen too many overconfident, untrained people go into a haunted house 'to clear it' and return with the spirit attached to them rather than 'banished' to the other world. If they have the kind of unresolved issues within their own being that we'll be looking at later in the book, they're especially open to such attachment. The same goes for the alien world. It's my experience that many of the 'alien encounters' people have are actually with hidden parts of their own psyche, although I'm not discounting that there's other life out there in the universe, nor that, if people are unwise enough to open themselves up to it, there may be interference and manipulation of life here on Earth by such beings. But personally, I'd rather stay away from that area unless I had no choice but to engage with it, and if I did, I'd want to know I had the right tools to hand to deal with it sensibly and effectively.

It's easy to get caught up in the prevailing zeitgeist or to enter more fully than you expect into the belief system or mindset of a book, film or fantasy. It's also easy to believe in something and actually create it – a thought form that takes on a life of its own.[3] Such a creation can feel all too real and can easily create havoc until dissolved. It can be used by discarnate spirits, too, so always check out any messages that are apparently being sent to you through channelling or clairvoyance. You should always thoroughly 'test the spirits'.

We also all have our inner demons and may sometimes be prey to feelings of vulnerability, self-blame, guilt and lack of confidence, or a bad case of 'poor me'. 'Poor me' victims experience a lack not only in finances but also in friends, resources, social opportunities, the job market and health, so it's not a happy frame of mind. There can be a part of ourselves that is at odds with the rest – what I have long dubbed the 'inner terrorist' – and that can wreak even more havoc than a terrorist in the outer world, as it makes us defensive, suspicious, aggressive and prone to attack ourselves and others rather than being healthily vulnerable and open where other people are concerned. But it doesn't need to be like this. The secret is in how you see yourself – and how quickly you turn a defeatist attitude into a positive one. Turn your attention elsewhere, put your intention on something positive, feel safe inside and your world changes.

Similarly, there are currents of negative energy out there, whether the thought or emotion streams of other people and their fears and expectations, or natural or man-made vibrations. Certain places have a bad atmosphere, literally 'bad vibes', or fall within the energetic pollution of electromagnetic or geomagnetic stress, and this can affect your well-being. Block these vibes from reaching you and your natural equilibrium returns. You may also, inadvertently or otherwise, trigger conscious or unconscious acrimonious or envious thoughts, either from someone else or, unrecognized, from your own self. And finally there are the vampires, those energy pirates who steal other people's energy to boost their own life, and the ill-wishers who are envious, angry or vindictive. Cut off these energy drains whilst holding forgiveness and compassion in your heart, and your own well-being is enhanced.

Many people believe psychic protection isn't for them because they haven't upset anyone or don't do anything 'weird' – by which they usually mean psychic. They assume that because they don't see ghosts or aren't consciously intuitive they're not open to the psychic realm. However, it can be in the small everyday things of life that psychic protection is most needed.

You may not realize how objects such as letters, photographs or gifts can tie you to someone after a relationship has finished, for instance. If there was any acrimony or power struggle in that relationship, the objects will still carry that charge. Even when the relationship finished on good terms, there might be hidden links. For this reason, it's wise to regularly clear out such things, either giving them away to a charity shop or jumble sale or recycling or burning them if this is more appropriate. If you really want to keep something, cleansing it with an appropriate essence (*see page 18*) or putting a crystal on it diminishes the possibility of anything still attaching to you through it – or of someone else holding on to a part of you or you to them. If you come under psychic attack from someone (*see pages 178–184*), it's essential to get rid of any gifts they gave you or objects belonging to them, as these are strong links through which they can reach you.

In fact, we could say it's all too easy to get caught up in negative energy. Working on this book, I'd been concentrating on writing Part II when I began to feel as though I was wading through treacle – a sign I am generating or in the presence of negative energy. I quickly turned my attention to Part III and the writing soon transmuted into a positive joy. Only when I felt completely anchored in that positive vibration was I able to return to the section on eliminating negativity. So, if you feel in need of a lift, it may help to move between sections as appropriate, but don't overlook the negative totally, as denial and repression create their own psychic mire.

Are You Giving your Energy Away?

If you're feeling exhausted, the physical, mental or emotional depletion you're suffering could be because you've given too much of yourself to someone else. Giving yourself away can occur at work, at play and in relationships. Whenever you become aware of being depleted after being with a particular person, ask yourself:

- 'Have I given away too much of my energy?'
- 'Did I detach when our contact finished?'
- 'Have I taken on negative energy or emotion?'
- 'Am I allowing this person to have undue influence over me?'
- 'Am I taking enough time for myself?'

You may also like to ask yourself:

- 'Do particular *places* affect me?' (If so, look at counteracting geopathic stress; *see pages xvii and 71*.)

- 'Do I get depleted when I travel on public transport?'
  (In which case, *see page xx*.)
- 'Do I always sit in the same place and feel tired?'
  (Check out geopathic and electromagnetic stress,
  pages xvii and 77.)

Throughout this book, you'll find ways of dealing with all these situations. For now, it's enough to have noted that this energy drop occurs and where and with whom it happens.

And What about your Boundaries?

If you have loose boundaries and are unable to say 'no' to people or resist their blandishments, psychic or otherwise, you could be in trouble, so ask yourself some questions about your boundaries:

- 'Am I able to say "no"?'
- 'Do I take on too much for others?'
- 'Do people come to me with their troubles?'
- 'Do I feel overwhelmed by people's emotions or thoughts?'
- 'Can I take "me time" without feeling guilty?'

If you aren't able to stand in your own space, *see page 58*. And if you aren't fully present in your body, some bodywork or yoga might be helpful in addition to the psychic self-protection you're giving yourself by working through this book.

How Do I Know Whether I Need Protection?

There are signs and signals that suggest you need self-protection and certain activities and states of mind in which it would be wise to protect yourself before undertaking any kind of intuitive activity:

Signs You May Need Psychic Self-Protection

- Do you read or watch programmes about sensational psychic activity?
- Are you meddling or dabbling in psychic things without being trained?
- Do you believe you're psychic or have a sixth sense?
- Do you meditate?
- Do you worry excessively about what is going on in the world?
- Are you obsessed with thoughts of failure or loss?
- Do things churn round and round in your mind?
- Have you got your head in the clouds?
- Do you use recreational drugs?
- Do people gravitate to you with their troubles?
- Do you give energy to other people?
- Does using a computer make you tired?
- Do certain people or places leave you feeling drained?
- Do you cry easily?
- Do you feel low if a friend is depressed or unhappy?
- Do you feel on edge if a friend is angry?
- Are you accident-prone?
- Have small things gone wrong recently?
- Do you lose things?
- Do you have nightmares and insomnia?
- Are you anxious, nervy, on edge?

- Do you have invisible feelers out, testing the air around you?
- Are you afraid to relax?
- Are you perpetually tired, listless, hopeless?
- Have you ever felt invaded, somehow *not yourself*?
- Do you feel someone 'has it in' for you?
- Were you born under the zodiac signs of Cancer, Scorpio or Pisces?
- Have you ever seen a ghost or felt 'bad vibes'?

Several of these signs taken together mean you're probably sensitive to energies and may need self-protection or are undertaking activities where it would be wise to protect yourself. All the water signs of the zodiac, Cancer, Scorpio and Pisces, tend to be naturally intuitive and easily pick things up, so they in particular need to learn about healthy boundaries, but everyone benefits from sensible protection.

Helping Yourself

This book contains practical easy-to-use solutions such as wearing or laying out crystals, putting yourself inside a light bubble, constructing a pyramid to create a safe space and, most importantly, changing the way you think and feel. These simple techniques can be used at any time and in any situation at home, work or play. There are also many other tools, including ceremony, journalling and visioning, that enhance your energy, provide protection when travelling, help you to develop inner strength and serenity, and more. All you have to do is remember to *use* the techniques – reading about them is all very well, but it won't do the job unless you also practise them, so that using them becomes an automatic process you don't even think about but simply apply as needed.

The book is structured so that you try out the basic tools first, move on to use them to remove negativity from yourself and your surroundings and then create a positive physical, mental, emotional and spiritual environment in which you can flourish.

Forever and Ever?

The beauty of having learned self-protection and dealt with your inner terrorist, toxic emotions and noxious thoughts is that it becomes an automatic process that kicks in whenever it's needed and you probably won't even notice it. By being grounded, feeling safe in your own skin and having a positive attitude, you will naturally be protected. Although you may need to stay vigilant under extreme circumstances, you'll have learned how to identify those and take the appropriate measures.

The best advice is that once you've cleared the past, let go of your fears, cut off the psychic vampires and found your security boundaries, you can forget about it and move on. Don't revisit the past or whatever you were afraid of, don't talk or think about it or give it any attention at all. Don't project your thoughts into the future and become fearful, just trust you are OK and stay in the present moment. *Feel* safe, maintain your positive outlook and you *are* protected – forever.

PART I
PROTECTION TOOLS

What Can I Do?

'Energy enhancement can come from a crystal, a flower essence, or the power of your own mind... A strong energy field and a positive outlook are the greatest life enhancers there are.'

Judy Hall, *Good Vibrations*

In this section you'll find quick and easy, tried and tested tools for creating protection for yourself and strengthening your energetic boundaries, together with a means of exploring how you really feel about your safety and the tools to overcome your fears and those of other people, if these are affecting you.

Some of these tools seem to be instinctive. People don't have to **learn** about crystals for instance, they just use them. A friend of mine, whose international wheeler-dealer husband has high-functioning Asperger's autism and is prone to anxiety attacks when faced with the unfamiliar, told me how he keeps a stone in his pocket. It's just a stone he picked up out of the gutter one day, a little brown rounded stone, nothing special to look at, but to him it represents security. He never goes anywhere without it and whenever he feels anxious he fondles it. It's the lifeline that takes him through traumatic times.

'I wish I had a little stone,' my friend said wistfully. I pointed out that all she had to do was look down at her feet as she stepped outside her door and she'd find one. Now she too has a little stone to anchor her to a safe world.

Five thousand years ago in Mesopotamia someone had a similar little round flat stone, but his was a slice of Agate inscribed in minute gold writing: 'Lord God Marduk, protect me.' No doubt he too felt safe when it was in his pocket. Amulets such as these have been used for thousands of years and are easy to create.

Safety starts with where you live and move and have your being, and being at home in your body with your feet firmly on the floor is the best protection of all. You can also use traditional protective devices that only take a few moments of your time and need no tool other than your mind's eye and a little imagination. Once you've experienced them, you'll know what it is to be fully self-protected, but there are many other tools we'll be using throughout this book, including crystals. By learning to use these tools and working through the 'Try this' exercises that accompany them you'll soon establish what feels good to you and what works best for the way in which you interact with the world.

SELF-PROTECTION TOOLS

All these tools are easy to use and build up into a useful self-protection kit. Approach this section in a spirit of fun and child-like pleasure in exploring something new, especially your shiny, sparkly crystal friends. After all, joy and happiness are some of the best forms of protection there are. Read through the sections on the tools, try the exercises and see which suits you.

The 'treasure chest' descriptions of crystals and the 'crystal tips' are to help you choose the right crystal for you. They're not essential for the exercises, although they build up into a multi-purpose crystal treasure chest if you select the ones that really resonate with you. I've given you my top ten favourites to get you started, together with ten of the very latest, new-generation crystal tools just coming onto the market that are perfect for the changing vibrations.

If a crystal produces instant strong antipathy, it can be a clue to something you're repressing at a deep level. Sitting quietly with such a stone and tuning in to what your body, feelings or thoughts are telling you, or writing without censorship in your journal, quickly brings the underlying cause to the surface and helps you to resonate with the crystal. But not every crystal is for everyone, so choose yours with care.

TOOL 1: YOUR CRYSTAL TREASURE CHEST

Your crystal treasure chest can contain a multitude of crystals or only one, and you don't even need to buy that. Any stone you pick up, such as a Flint pebble or a water-tumbled Milk Quartz or Jasper, can be imbued with intent and protective energy and work as well as an expensive crystal. Anything that catches your eye is the stone for you – as long as you remember the simple rules of cleanse, energize, programme, use and cleanse again.

It will undoubtedly be considered heresy by crystal purists who set great store by the unique properties of specific crystals, but any crystal (throughout this book any stone is referred to as a crystal, regardless of whether it's a gem quality or semi-precious stone or a lump of rock) does anything you ask it to – provided you do ask. So one stone could be used for everything, although once you begin to work with crystals you soon realize that having several to choose from widens what you can do with them, as otherwise you can overload a stone.

Overleaf are my top ten treasure chest 'essential favourites' and also a list of ten new-generation, high-vibration stones. The essential top ten are all you'll need, although you can have fun trying the other stones in the treasure chests throughout the book, choosing one or two to enhance your protection experience. My own particular favourites are a Brandenberg Amethyst and a piece of Shungite.

Beautiful crystals are lovely to look at and stunning to wear, but crystals don't have to be beautiful to be effective. Some of the most powerful stones are also some of the ugliest – to the casual, external eye. When you learn to see with your inner eye, you glimpse their power and their inner beauty.

If you are getting together a crystal treasure chest it can be useful to have a range of colours and shapes and a combination of earthy and high-vibration stones. Long, pointed crystals focus energy into a specific place, drawing positive energy down into your body if placed point in, or releasing negativity if placed point out. Round and tumbled crystals gently radiate energy.

In recent times brown and smoky crystals have been used for the earth energy centre beneath your feet, red and orange crystals for the creative energy centres (your lower chakras) in your belly, yellow for the emotional centre in your solar plexus, green or pink for the heart centre, blue for the throat, indigo-purple for the third eye and lilac or white for the crown. A set of multi-coloured crystals can cleanse, align and boost these energy centres, but you can also choose crystals for specific purposes such as reversing negative earth energies (geopathic stress) or overcoming electromagnetic emanations.

Treasure Chest

ROSE QUARTZ

Known as the stone of unconditional love and forgiveness, gentle Rose Quartz opens the heart and transforms negative emotions into positive ones. It's an excellent stone to use during crisis or trauma, as it quickly brings peace. It transmutes negative emotional conditioning and supports positive affirmations.

Top Ten Treasure Chest Favourites

- *Amazonite:* A useful protector against electromagnetic stress, this calming stone is a powerful filter (*see page 74*).
- *Amber:* One of the most ancient of protections for the aura, this stone cleanses your aura and draws spiritual energies down into your body (*see page 206*).
- *Amethyst:* Traditionally used to overcome being too open, Amethyst assists in safely accessing the higher dimensions (*see page 22*).
- *Aventurine:* Useful if other people draw on your energy, this stone is also an attractor of prosperity (*see page 122*).
- *Black Tourmaline:* Turns back ill-wishing and protects against psychic mugging, electromagnetic or geopathic stress, or negative energy of any kind (*see page 184*).
- *Celestite:* Wear Celestite to connect to your guardian angel and the highest spiritual vibrations (*see page 45*).
- *Labradorite:* An excellent protective stone that opens your psychic abilities and helps you to maintain joyful connection with divine energy (*see page xiii*).
- *Rose Quartz:* The stone of unconditional love that heals your heart (*see page 7*).
- *Selenite:* Crystallized divine light, Selenite is the interface between spirit and matter (*see page 99*).
- *Smoky Quartz:* A powerful cleanser of negative energy, ideal for gridding and grounding (*see page 16*).

Top Ten New Generation High-Vibration Crystals

- *Brandenberg Amethyst:* This stone holds the perfect blueprint of all that could be. It heals at every level and facilitates ancestral, earth and personal release (*see page 21*).
- *Eye of the Storm:* This stone keeps you calm and centred in your heart no matter what may be going on around you (*see page 29*).
- *Green Ridge Quartz:* With its wide spectrum of energies, Green Ridge Quartz is an excellent way to cleanse and recharge your system and open the higher chakras (*see page 66*).
- *Nunderite:* This stone is an excellent grounding stone. It provides a calm, still centre in which to anchor your energies (*see page 48*).
- *Polychrome Jasper:* An amazing energy shield and 'stone of happiness' (*see page 184*).
- *Preseli Bluestone:* Crystallized earth energy, this stone is a combination of extremely earthly vibrations that connect you deeply into the Earth with the ability to contact the highest levels and journey through multi-dimensions (*see page 38*).
- *Rainbow Mayanite:* The ultimate tool for tie-cutting and consciousness expansion (*see page 123*).
- *Richterite:* Although high vibration, Richterite's greatest power lies in assisting the body to withstand constant stress or sudden trauma (*see page 43*).
- *Shungite:* The most phenomenal shielding power of them all (*see page 73*).
- *Tantalite:* This stone soaks up negative energy and guards against psychic vampirism or environmental

pollution. A powerful cleanser of negative energy, ideal for gridding and grounding (*see page 13*).

Treasure Chest

LEMURIAN SEED QUARTZ

A Lemurian crystal makes an excellent wand as it is a naturally long, extended point. It unites the physical and subtle levels of being, helps us to remember our spiritual selves, and grounds vibrational shifts into the physical body. The etched markings can be ascended like a ladder to access multi-dimensional levels. Lemurians remind lightworkers to attend to their evolution as well as facilitating that of others. Lemurian wands are excellent for chakra balancing and clearing, especially for removing karmic debris and soul imperatives. Activating the 'higher resonance' of each chakra, they integrate it with the lightbody.

Crystal Tips for Personal Self-Protection
Amber, Apache Tear, Aquamarine, Black Tourmaline, Bronzite, Citrine, Hematite, Nuummite, Smoky Quartz.

Try This
Check if you already own a crystal, or indeed several. Can you name them and do you know their properties? (If not check them out in *The Crystal Bibles*.) Have them standing by.

> • *Ill-wishing:* Conscious or unconscious acrimonious or envious thoughts directed to someone else or, unrecognized, your own self.

Choosing your Crystal(s)

You possibly already have some favourite crystals but may want to acquire more – they can be addictive. We've already touched on picking up a pebble that appeals to you but, faced with the enormous choice in a crystal shop, how do you go about choosing? Well, you can do it the rational way: read the lists given in this book or glance through *The Crystal Bibles*, identify the stones that have the properties you're seeking, see which picture attracts you and go out and buy that stone. Or you can do it the irrational way: plunging your hand into a group of crystals in a shop. That way you usually come up with one or two that are for you, or your eye alights on one instantly. That's the intuitive way to choose your crystal, to let it call to you. If you do that, you often find yourself going home with something different from what you thought you were going to buy, but find it's the perfect crystal for you.

> • *Chakra:* An energy centre linking the physical body and the aura.

Try This

Next time you're out walking, look around for a pebble that could become 'your crystal' or 'your guidestone'. Water-rounded Milk Quartz, Flint,

Jasper or other pebbles are ideal as they are very tactile. Keep this crystal with you at all times. But that's not the end of the story. If your crystal is to work on your behalf you need to ask it to do what you require – and you need to cleanse and recharge it before doing anything else.

Cleaning, Charging and Programming your Crystals

As crystals readily absorb vibrations of all kinds and pick up the energies of everyone and anything who handles them or is around them, they need to be cleansed regularly, especially before being used for the first time. They will benefit from regular cleaning even if you only wear them as jewellery or have them on display.

Cleaning your crystals is simple if you choose tumbled stones or single points. You merely have to hold them under running water for a few minutes and, preferably, put them out in the sun and possibly the moon to recharge (white crystals are particularly fond of moonlight). If sunlight isn't available, you can put them onto a large Quartz cluster or Carnelian to recharge. You can also use salt water to cleanse robust stones. If you use crystal clusters or stones that are fragile or dissolve, such as Selenite or Halite, the crystals need placing in raw brown rice overnight.

Once a crystal has been cleaned and energetically recharged, it needs programming to ensure that it is working in harmony with you and in accord with your intention. (The reason crystals sometimes don't work for people is they often forget to ask!) The first time you programme a crystal, hold it in your hands and ask it to always work for your highest good and that of others. If you want it to do something specific, like form a shield of protection, be precise but don't limit it. If you add 'and whatever else this crystal can do for me' it opens up exciting new possibilities.

Try This
Crystal Balance Crystal Cleanser and Crystal Recharge, Petaltone Clear2Light and Crystal Charge will cleanse and replenish your crystals.

Treasure Chest

TANTALITE
Tantalite soaks up negative energy and guards against psychic vampirism or environmental pollution. It creates an energetic grid around the body to 'repel boarders'. Clearing the effect of psychic attack or ill-wishing, Tantalite removes hooks, attachments, implants, mental imperatives and core beliefs lodged in the etheric or physical body, in the present or previous lives, that create dis-ease and vulnerability. Grid or wear to deflect geopathogens, radiation and other adverse energies.

Treasure Chest

HALITE

Halite is an efficient cleanser of energy. It dissolves negative thoughts, reframes old patterns and assists in turning around ingrained feelings such as anger, abandonment or rejection, promoting emotional well-being. It dissolves on contact with water and can be used in the bath or shower or gridded around a room. Other crystals can be placed on it to purify them. It's particularly useful if you become the object of someone else's unreasonable lust or needy feelings.

Try This

Give all your crystals, stones and jewellery an energetic cleanse and recharge now and ask them to work with you for your highest good.

Crystal Tip

Placing crystals on Halite cleanses them and a large Quartz cluster or a Red Carnelian quickly cleanses and recharges crystals when sunlight is unavailable.

TOOL 2: CRYSTAL LAYOUTS

When crystals are laid out in specific shapes their innate energy is channelled not only through the crystal lattice from which they are formed but also by the way the shapes themselves compel energy to move (**see Tool 20,**

Traditional Symbols for suggested shapes). Spirals radiate energy while squares contain it, and hexagrams or pentagrams draw positive energy into the shape and release negative energy.

You can lay stones around yourself or create a shape within a room or your house (*see Creating Safe Space, page 71*), or lay a permanent grid in your garden with rough stones that won't weather (the colour may fade but the layout will remain effective).

Try This

Lay 12 cleansed stones in a spiral, starting from the middle and moving out to the edge. Put your hand over the spiral and feel how it generates and spreads energy outwards, with the energy radiating out from the last stone.

Now form the same crystals into a square. Put your hand over the middle of the square and to one side of the square, and feel how it contains the energy, keeping it within the shape (*see pages 14–15* for crystal layouts).

TOOL 3: AMULETS

Amulets are crystals that have been specifically programmed to protect the wearer or to attract prosperity. Traditionally they were tied around the upper arm or the neck and were often inscribed with a picture of a god and a plea for protection or with astrological signs or protective symbols.

Treasure Chest

SMOKY QUARTZ

One of the major stones for drawing off or blocking negative energy, Smoky Quartz is an excellent antidote to stress or worry. It fortifies your resolve and supports you in letting go of any patterns you no longer need. It also grounds you in your body and assists you in accepting physical incarnation.

SMOKY ELESTIAL QUARTZ

Smoky Elestial Quartz has a much higher vibration than Smoky Quartz. It stabilizes and cleanses energy and is perfect for anchoring a grid, or your body, into incarnation. It transmutes energy into light and helps you to journey safely through multi-dimensions.

Try This

Holding in your hands the pebble you picked up, or an amulet crystal, ask that it be imbued with protection. You can address this plea to God, or to one of the traditional gods such as Marduk (the planet Jupiter, who also brings prosperity), or to your guardian angel, or simply to your own higher being. Keep the crystal with you at all times.

Crystal Tips

Traditional amulet crystals include Carnelian, Jasper, Quartz and precious gems.

TOOL 4: RELAXATION CRYSTALS

Regular relaxation conveys enormous benefit to your well-being and crystals can be particularly useful in helping you to achieve the relaxed but focused state that is particularly conducive to journeying and vision work. Inducing a deep sense of calm and centredness, crystals quieten your body, mind and emotions and help you to unwind.

Try This: Crystal Relaxation Layout

- Lie down and make yourself comfortable. Ensure you won't be disturbed. Turn off your phone.
- Place Smoky Quartz at your feet, focusing on your intention to relax.
- Place Yellow Jasper over your solar plexus.
- Place Rose Quartz over your heart.
- Place Blue Lace Agate at your throat.
- Place Amethyst on your forehead.
- Place Clear Quartz above your head.
- Close your eyes, breathe gently and leave the crystals in place for 15 minutes.
- Remove the crystals, starting with the top of your head. When you get to your feet, be aware of the grounding cord going from your feet deep into the Earth.

Crystal Tips for Relaxation

- *Amethyst: A natural tranquillizer that induces a profound sense of peace and relaxation and shuts off mind chatter.*

- *Blue Lace Agate:* The serene energies of this stone induce a profound peace of mind and link you to higher guidance.
- *Green Aventurine:* Imparts a sense of well-being and emotional serenity.
- *Smoky Quartz:* Instils a deep sense of relaxation into the physical body.
- *Nunderite:* helps the body to remain calm and relaxed during trauma.

TOOL 5: GEM ESSENCES

Gem essences have been used for thousands of years and they are an excellent way to imbibe the energy of a crystal and to treat the underlying mental or emotional causes of dis-ease. The ancients would leave a stone out overnight and collect the dew imbued with the essence of that stone. It's still really simple to make a gem essence today. Remember to focus your intention as you do so.

Try This: Making a Gem Essence
<u>You will need:</u>
- a clean glass bowl(s)
- crystal(s)
- spring water
- a funnel or small jug
- a clean glass bottle
- brandy, vodka or cider vinegar.

Making the Essence:

- Choose your crystal treasure chests or crystal tips and cleanse them thoroughly.
- Pour a small amount of spring water into a clean glass bowl and immerse the crystals in it. If a crystal is at all toxic or fragile (for example, Tantalite, Bumble Bee Jasper, Selenite, Angel's Wing Calcite or Malachite), you'll need an extra glass bowl in which to place the crystal within the water.
- Stand the glass bowl, water and crystal in the sun for several hours (white stones like to go out under the moon too).
- Remove the crystals and carefully pour the gem essence into the clean glass bottle. Fill with two-thirds brandy. Label and date. Keep in a cool dark place.
- You have made a mother essence and this can either be used by adding a few drops to a glass of spring water and sipping throughout the day or rubbing on your skin or adding to your bath, or you can make a dosage bottle by adding a few drops to one-third brandy and two-thirds spring water in a small dropper bottle to take regularly. You can also spray gem essences around the room or on your pillow.

TOOL 6: JOURNALLING

Keeping a record of your experiences not only increases your insights and your confidence but also charts your progress and shows you which tools work best for you. Use a special journal and write as fully as possible.

The silly little things you don't think have any meaning may well turn out to be crucial and small snippets may one day add up to a big insight.

Journalling is particularly useful for catching yourself having negative thoughts or black feelings, fears or worries. Write as freely as you can and you'll soon identify them. And when you can find the opposite, positive quality, write it in your journal and use it as an affirmation or positive thought (*see Tools 13 and 16*).

Try This

Buy yourself a special journal and write something when you go to bed every night for a week. You may also find it helpful to wake a few minutes early to record your dreams or a 'stream of consciousness' that simply flows off the pen and onto the paper without censoring anything. Read it through and highlight anything you weren't aware of or any fears or positive insights you have. Be sure to turn negative thoughts or emotions into positive qualities and record these in your journal.

TOOL 7: THE BUBBLE OF LIGHT

The bubble of light is one of the oldest forms of self-protection, used in all cultures and times, and I make no apologies for suggesting it again here. A quick and easy form of visioning (*see page 37*), it can be extended through the use of a crystal such as Quartz, Amethyst or Amber (*see page 206*). It's particularly helpful when you have to enter a crowd of people and you may also find specific people invoke a desire to safeguard your energy in this way (in which case, *see page 97*). Once you've identified who brings up this need, you can put your light bubble around yourself before you need it. However, the most sensible thing to do is to start the day by ensuring your bubble is in place and then keep it there throughout the day. If you've used a crystal to create the bubble, wear or carry the crystal with you.

Treasure Chest

BRANDENBERG AMETHYST

Found only at a sacred site in Namibia, a Brandenberg is a multi-purpose tool that looks after your energies on so many levels. It holds the perfect blueprint of pure energy before anything else became imprinted on it and so can restore your vibrations to pristine condition. It removes karmic encrustations, ancestral patterns, toxic emotions, mental dross and so much besides.

A portal to expanded awareness and a tool for spiritual alchemy, its inner planes and bubbles take you travelling in safety through multi-dimensional reality. A gatekeeper that protects against psychic attack and alien invasion, it repels negative energy by calling in positive light. Brandenberg holds a light when working in shadows or the underworld, and facilitates purification and integration of your present self. A Smoky Brandenberg is an extraordinarily powerful earth-healing tool.

Treasure Chest

AMETHYST

A natural tranquillizer, Amethyst de-stresses and protects you on all levels and provides emotional balance. It is useful for blocking geopathic stress and negative or noxious energies. Sitting quietly holding it will calm your mind and allow you to access the deeper parts of yourself to gain insight and find new motivation.

Try This

Using the power of your mind, picture a bubble of light at arm's length around your body, making sure it goes over your head, under your feet and behind your back (you may find it easiest to start with holding a torch over your head and bringing this down around your body, working towards your feet). Make sure the light bubble goes behind your back and under your feet and seals itself there. For extra self-protection, see yourself standing inside a large hollow crystal filled with light.

Crystal Tip

A tumbled Clear Quartz or any other egg-shaped crystal is ideal for maintaining and reminding you of your light bubble. Crystal eggs gently nurture and gestate new ideas or emotions.

Treasure Chest

QUARTZ

The most prevalent crystal on the planet, Quartz is excellent for amplifying, unblocking and generating energy, cleansing and healing the body and other crystals, storing information and heightening perception in addition to forming a protective barrier that negative energies cannot cross. All the different forms of Quartz provide excellent psychic protection and most enhance your ability to raise your awareness and open your higher chakras.

TOOL 8: THE GOLDEN PYRAMID

Pyramids are another ancient form of protection that create a safe space and provide protection for you or your home or workplace. A pyramid is one of the sacred symbols traditionally used to create sacred space (*see page 41*).

When creating your pyramid, remember it needs a floor as well as the four sides that meet at the apex. A shiny golden pyramid is particularly useful, as it bounces negative energy off the sides (you can also picture a 'negativity collector' that collects the negative energy and sends it to a great energy recycling plant in the sky) and shines light into the centre.

If you find it difficult to picture a pyramid in your mind's eye, you can create one from any kind of crystal, metal or gold-coloured card. Remember to build your pyramid with focused intention (*see Tool 11*).

In certain situations a green pyramid can be used (*see page 117*). You can support your visualization by using an actual crystal pyramid.

Treasure Chest

RUTILATED QUARTZ

Rutilated Quartz, also known as Angel's Hair, has strands of golden Rutile embedded within the Clear Quartz to amp up the energy even further. A spiritual stone, it provides an energy shield, cleanses space and draws off dis-ease of all kinds. It's particularly useful when you wish to make a change of direction or get to the root of a problem. It efficiently disposes of fears and induces a positive outlook.

Try This

Picture a golden pyramid that completely encloses your space, be it a house, a flat, a room such as an office, or yourself (in which case you may need to picture wheels on the four corners so that it moves with you). The pyramid has four sides and a floor. Use bright golden light coming down from the apex to sweep out the inside of the pyramid so it's clean and fresh. Finally, picture a revolving golden sphere suspended near the apex, sending out golden light into your space and constantly replenishing positive energy – placing Golden Quartz in your environment is an excellent way to facilitate this.

Treasure Chest

GOLDEN QUARTZ

Golden Quartz is found in several forms and has fantastic healing and protective energy. It is perfect for rituals that provide you with protection and enhance your well-being, raising both your psychic and physical immune system to optimum.

- *Dis-ease:* A state of disharmony and disequilibrium that can lead to physical, emotional, mental or psychic disease.

TOOL 9: BREATHING

Breathing is one of the most important ways of anchoring yourself in your body and distributing energy around that body. Shallow breathing is a symptom of chronic anxiety and stress and creates energetic holes in your aura through which outside vibrations can affect you or your own energy can be sucked out. If you don't pull the breath deep down inside your lungs, you're only half in your body. As a result, you're ungrounded – and that's an unsafe place to be.

When you're frightened or anxious, the tendency is to hold your breath. So, whenever you feel panicky, disorientated or light-headed, take a few moments to do the exercise that follows. It soon becomes automatic, and the more you do it, the more firmly grounded in your body you become – and the more energized.

Treasure Chest

JASPER

Jasper is found in many colours and forms and is excellent for energizing, de-stressing, journeying (*see page 53*) and blocking environmental pollution. This stone imparts strong determination and quick thinking and balances all the levels of your being.

STROMATOLITE OR KAMBABA JASPER

The fossilized remains of two of the oldest forms of life on the planet, Stromatolite and Kambaba Jasper (Green Stromatolite) may well have been responsible for the oxygenation of Earth's atmosphere. Useful grounding and protective stones, they help you to breathe deep into the centre of your being, grounding yourself here on the Earth. Kambaba Jasper goes right to your foundations bringing stability - physically and of purpose. It harmonizes you with the cycles of the natural world, attuning your personal biorhythm to that of the planet.

Try This: Belly Breathing

- Stand or sit with your feet firmly on the floor and your knees relaxed.
- Letting your shoulders hang loose, take a long, slow breath. Deliberately push out your ribs and belly and pull the breath deep into the base of your lungs. Feel your ribs expanding outwards at the back and sides and your back and solar plexus opening up.
- Breathe in for a count of four (increase the count with practice), hold the breath for a count of two and exhale slowly, pulling your belly and ribs in to expel all the air for a count of ten. Press your ribs in with your hands to assist.
- Rest a moment and take another breath.
- Repeat eight times more (stop immediately if you feel light-headed and take your attention down to your feet, bouncing firmly on the Earth).
- Return to your normal breathing pattern, but remember to pull the air deep down into your lungs.

Crystal Tip

Keep an earthy stone such as a Flint pebble or tumbled Jasper, Kambaba Jasper, Stromatolite, Eye of the Storm or Hematite in your hip pocket to pull the breath deep into your belly.

TOOL 10: GETTING GROUNDED

If you're ungrounded, floaty and 'space cadet-ish', or live in your head or with your head in the clouds, you're unlikely to feel safe in your body. Nor, strangely enough, are you likely to feel safe if you're aware of nothing but your body. You need to be sensibly aware of the outside world and the spiritual dimensions *and* be grounded in your body. Being fully grounded is one of the best forms of self-protection there is.

Treasure Chest

FLINT

Flint is a common stone, especially in chalky soil. Much prized for Stone Age technology such as axes and arrowheads, as a ritual item or attractive stone, it was buried with the dead to protect their souls and guide them to the next world. It is an excellent stone for earthing and grounding, drain cutting (*see page 118*) and energy transmitting and stabilizing.

Try This

To ground yourself instantly, stamp your feet.

Grounding works particularly well with bare feet on grass or earth. This really anchors you to the Earth. Brown crystals such as Flint, Hematite, Smoky Quartz, Eye of the Storm or Boji stones also keep you grounded. Keep one in your pocket if you have a tendency to float off the planet.

Another effective way of grounding yourself is to imagine that you're connected to a root that goes deep into the centre of the Earth. This technique has been used in shamanic cultures for many years and shamans tend to take the root from the base of the spine. However, having the root coming out of your feet also helps you to remain upright and secure in your body (although you can use both or either).

Remember to re-establish your root after visioning or journeying exercises (*see pages 37 and 53*) or whenever you feel floaty and spaced out.

Treasure Chest

EYE OF THE STORM (JUDY'S JASPER)

A brand new find and powerful heart-healer, Eye of the Storm does exactly what the name suggests: it provides you with a calm, safe refuge during times of change or turmoil. It protects your energies, transmutes negativity and helps you to gain objective insights into what is going on. Wear it as a protective shield or keep it in your environment for maximum benefit.

Try This: Establishing your Root

- Stand or sit with your feet firmly on the floor and take your attention down to your feet. Close your eyes.
- Picture a root protruding from the bottom of each of your feet. A metre or so below your feet

the two roots entwine to form a thicker root. This root then passes deep down into the Earth, where it joins the molten core and is able to channel energy up into your body to energize and protect you.

• Feel this energy travelling up to your legs to the base of your spine and up your spine to the top of your head.

The root is flexible and allows you to move around, but it holds you firmly grounded in your physical body.

If you're a touchy-feely (kinaesthetic) person, try massaging the centre of the soles of your feet with a crystal until they tingle and then placing them firmly on the Earth with a grounding crystal between them. Dravide (Brown) Tourmaline, Eye of the Storm, Flint, Preseli Bluestone or Smoky Quartz help to establish your root when placed on or between your feet.

Crystal Tips for Grounding

Amber, Aragonite, Boji Stones, Bronzite, Brown Elestial Quartz, Dalmatian Stone, Dravide (Brown) Tourmaline, Eye of the Storm, Flint, Fire Agate, Hematite, Kambaba Jasper, Red and Brown Jasper, Smoky Quartz, Stromatolite.

TOOL 11: INTENTION AND FOCUS

The power of your mind to create is a truly awesome thing – when you consciously use it. Actually, it's pretty awesome when you don't consciously use it, but then it just creates the wrong kind of things and you keep wondering why life doesn't work out as you planned.

Where you put your focus and how you use your intention are crucial if you're to feel safe. Where you put your focus affects what you perceive and this in turn to a large extent creates your world. If you focus on the negative, that is what you see. But if you focus on the positive, that is what transpires. And intention is focused thought. It's what you want to bring about. It is one of the most potent tools you have for changing your world. Therefore you need to ensure your intention is focused in a positive direction, creating fundamental security rather than chasing after things you feel would make you happy, secure or whatever.

Use the power of intention to change your mindset and your worldview and suddenly all possibilities become open. This is the power-full ancient principle of 'like attracts like' and also of 'do as you would be done by'. If your unselfish intention is to be of benefit to others as well as yourself, the universe is happy to cooperate with you.

Focusing your attention into an exercise and holding the positive intent that it manifests is the easiest way possible, with right timing, and finally letting go of that intent helps you to bring about the desired outcome. Crystals are an excellent receptacle for intention as they continue to manifest it for you once you've let it go.

Intention has to work in harmony with right timing – there is no point in trying to push against the river, and worrying about when it will manifest is counter-productive and simply stops the flow. So, when you've formulated your intention, go with the flow. Trust that things will happen with right timing in the correct way for your highest good and that you cannot always know when or how that will be, but it will be absolutely right when it happens. And when it does manifest, remember to use the power of gratitude to thank the universe for cooperating with you.

Sometimes your intention cannot manifest because there is interference from your subconscious mind. It's rather like a computer program running in the background that overloads the system because it's in direct conflict and keeps trying to shut the new program down. This old program is usually a negative belief you carry or an outworn emotion you are holding on to, but someone else's belief that something would be good for you can also interfere if they have a strong enough mind. Interference can also arise from feeling you *ought* to do something, or be a certain way, or whatever, but secretly still holding on to how you are because you're scared of change. Fortunately a crystal protects you against this.

Becoming aware of the hidden programs you're running is essential if you're to work with intention in the most constructive way possible. If you try to make a conscious decision whilst running an unconscious program, what will inevitably manifest is that deeper desire. So, if things aren't working out quite how you expect, explore what your own deepest intent actually is and transform that into something positive (*see Crystal EFT, page 130*).

Try to remember, even when I don't remind you, to carry out all the actions in this book with focused intention. It will enhance their effectiveness triplefold.

Treasure Chest

IRON PYRITE

A useful energy shield, Iron Pyrite is excellent for harnessing your intention and creating positive change. It enables you to tap into your unrecognized potential and have confidence in your abilities.

Try This: Framing your Intention

Think about your intention of feeling safe and using the tools in this book to create inner security. Make your intention as specific as possible and phrase it in the present tense – it's more potent that way. Make it as precise and succinct as possible. Hold your intention crystal in your hands and state your intention out loud, programming it into the crystal. Place your crystal where it will remind you of your intention.

Crystal Tips for Supporting Intention

Brandenberg Amethyst, Desert Rose, Manifestation Crystal (a crystal that has a smaller crystal completely contained within it), Phantom Quartz, Rose Quartz, square Iron Pyrite, Topaz, Watermelon Tourmaline.

TOOL 12: TRUST

Trust in yourself and in the process of living that you are going through is a vital part of psychic self-protection. After all, if you don't trust yourself, whom can you trust and, perhaps more to the point, who will trust you? You need to trust that you can change your attitude, meet changes with confidence and feel inwardly safe. And you need to trust the guidance your inner self gives you and to follow the process without over-analysing.

Treasure Chest

SMITHSONITE

A harmonious and tranquil stone, Smithsonite promotes trust in yourself and the universe, releasing stress and supporting you when you feel at breaking point or unloved. It gently dissolves emotional pain and infuses you with well-being. This is the perfect stone for gridding (*see page 89*) around your bed to support your immune system, both physical and psychic. It's also useful for ascertaining the truth of intuitive communication and insight.

However, this level of trust isn't about naïvety or gullibility. Nor is it about taking everything as absolute truth. You also need to check in with yourself to see what your inner being or your body says. The least bit of squirming in your stomach or doubt in your mind needs checking out. You also need to use your common sense and ability to discriminate. If trust in yourself is lacking at a deep level, you'll constantly meet people and circumstances that abuse and misuse your trust. You also need to trust the guidance you're given from your unseen helpers and angels and from the universe – and remember that these beings are there for you when you need help.

And finally, you need to trust that the situation in which you find yourself is right for you at this time as it is helping you to establish your own inner sense of rightness and develop your personal power. If you cultivate a mindset of absolute trust that whatever is for your highest good happens, it is so.

Treasure Chest

PORPHYRITE

Restoring trust in your Higher Self, your inner self, your soul and other people, Porphyrite encourages you to speak your truth no matter how afraid you may be. It helps you listen to and trust your inner guidance and teaches you that real truth comes from deep within your soul. It also assists you to deal with ancestral issues that have passed down the family line, especially where these involve family secrets and lies.

Try This
Ask yourself, on a scale of one to ten, 'How much trust do I have in the tools in this book right now?'

If your score was low, hold the intention: 'I allow trust to develop as I find the right tools for myself. 'If your score was high, you're well on the way to developing a high level of self-protection.

Crystal Tips for Enhancing Trust
Amber, Chrysoprase, Labradorite, Lemurian Gold Opal, Pink Chalcedony, Porphyrite, Rose Quartz, Sapphire, Smithsonite, Sodalite, Tremolite, Tugtupite.

TOOL 13: AFFIRMATIONS

Affirmations are closely linked to trust and use the power of intention to bring a desired outcome to fruition or to reverse a negative expectation. When you've decided what you want to bring into being, writing it down and phrasing it in the most positive way possible in the present tense ensures it manifests in the *now*. Say it out loud, repeat it several times and let yourself feel all the feelings attached: joy, safety, security, love. The more intensely you can feel these feelings, the stronger the manifestation will be. Looking yourself in the eye in a mirror also assists with affirmations. Smiling as you do so boosts their effectiveness 200 per cent. Then let go.

Crystals make the perfect receptacle for affirmations. Simply place the crystal with your affirmation in the environment and leave it to do its work. One of the secrets of effective affirmations is, once you've said them with all the feelings and intention possible, then to let them go. The more you can leave them to manifest without giving them attention or worrying about the outcome, the more effective the affirmation is.

TOOL 14: VISIONING AND RE-VISIONING

'Visioning' means 'seeing with the inner eye'. It uses the powers of imagination and intention and the ability of the mind to create or recall images, but you don't need to actually see a picture to use visioning as a creation tool. Some people *feel* or *sense* rather than see. The trick is to act as though you're seeing, to make the experience feel as real as possible by using all your senses and harnessing your emotions.

To help open your mind's eye, close your eyes and look up to the point above and between your eyebrows. This activates your third eye. You may see a 'screen' which opens as your third eye opens, or you may find your visioning occurs a few feet in front of you or all around you. Certain crystals (see below) are particularly good for opening the third eye. Place them on your forehead.

Treasure Chest

EMERALD

Traditionally associated with Venus, the planet of love, Emerald was used for amulets to attract good relationships or to ward off enchantments. It's a stone of equilibrium on all levels and imparts the strength of character to overcome misfortune, assisting in regeneration. A wisdom stone, it also helps to discern truth.

Treasure Chest

PRESELI BLUESTONE

Traditionally a powerful personal and earth-healing stone, Preseli Bluestone ensures that you always maintain your direction and your core strength. It helps to orientate you within your world and keeps you fully grounded.
This powerful stone assists in staying 'in the moment' and yet assists in journeying through the shamanic worlds or through multi-dimensions.

Try This

To convince yourself that you can indeed see with your mind's eye, close your eyes and imagine a bright shiny apple. When you bite into it, it's sharp and sour. Feel how your mouth puckers, even though you know it's going to be sour.

Crystal Tips for Opening the Third Eye

Apophyllite, Azurite with Malachite, Blue Selenite, Bytownite, Clear or Phantom Quartz, Golden Labradorite, Green Ridge Quartz, Iolite, Petalite, Prehnite, Preseli Bluestone, Rhomboid Calcite.

Re-visioning

'Re-visioning' is slightly different from 'visioning'. It means taking a situation from the past and reviewing it in a different light, creating it again but more positively.

With re-visioning, rather than seeing the negatives in a situation, you look for the gifts you received and the lessons you learned and then apply them to creating your future. You literally see the experience again in a new light by re-visioning the whole thing.

Treasure Chest

APOPHYLLITE

A useful stone for opening the third eye, Apophyllite assists journeying (*see pages 53–55*) and intuition. It facilitates introspection, seeks out the causes of dis-ease or fear and releases negative thought patterns.

BYTOWNITE

The yellow form of Labradorite, placing Bytownite on the third eye opens and expands your awareness clearing any blockages. Accessing the highest levels of consciousness, it facilitates visualisation and attunes you to higher wisdom. Bytownite detaches you from undue influence by others.

Try This: Re-visioning the Past

In your journal write up one of the worst experiences of your life, how you felt and the negative thought patterns that have arisen from that. See if you can identify any positive gifts that you gained from the experience.

Then turn the situation around by going back to the start of the experience and, with the benefit of hindsight and the positive gifts or skills you learned, literally reframing it. See it turning out completely differently. Use the power of your mind to visualize it as one of the best experiences of your life. See yourself making all the right moves and decisions, and things going your way. Let yourself feel all the emotions of that re-visioning and bring that success into the present moment. Bask in how it feels to have re-visioned that situation, to have made it your own.

TOOL 15: CEREMONY

Ceremony and ritual are other ancient tools that harness your mind and honour your intention. When carrying out a ceremony, it's usual to do this within a cleansed sacred space (*see overleaf*). Some people like to wear a robe, but this isn't necessary. It does make a ceremony feel special if you take the time to have a bath or shower and put on clean clothes, but even this isn't essential. It's more important that you carry out the ceremony seriously but joyfully, with your attention and emotions fully engaged. Music can assist the process, as can candles and incense, but, as with everything, it's your intention and focus that bring success.

Treasure Chest

ELESTIAL QUARTZ

Known as the stone of the angels, Elestial Quartz is perfect for opening and maintaining sacred space. Acting as an emotional transformer dissolving confusion, blockages and fear, it serves as a catalyst for necessary change – which may come about abruptly. Different colours of Elestial Quartz also have specific functions, Smoky Elestial being an effective energy cleanser and blocker, while White Elestial draws angels and high-frequency spiritual energy to you and Rose Quartz Elestial is one of the finest heart healers and love-enhancers of them all.

Try This: Creating Sacred Space Ceremony

- Cleanse your space appropriately (*see pages 55 and 72*) and stand facing south.
- Place a small bowl of water on the ground and call in the guides and guardians of that direction to assist you in creating sacred space, saying, 'May the gods and guardians of the south, in whatever form they take, assist me to create sacred space through the power of the water element.'
- Turn to the west and place a crystal on the ground, calling in the guides and guardians of that direction, through the power of the earth element.

- In the north, place a feather and once more call in the guardians through the power of the air element.
- In the east, place a lighted candle and call in the guides through the power of the fire element.
- Stand in the centre of the circle, in the place of Above and Below and All that Is, and call in the energies of Father Sun and Mother Earth to assist you.
- Use the directions circle you have created for journeying, meditation, visioning, healing, ceremony or any other purpose for which a safe, sacred space is required.
- When you dismantle the circle, as you remove the items marking it, thank the guides and guardians of that direction for their assistance.

Crystal Tip

A large piece of Elestial or Rose Quartz or Selenite makes an excellent altar centrepiece that holds sacred space.

TOOL 16: POSITIVE THOUGHT

Change is inevitable, but for some people it's an exciting challenge and for others it's an unbearable stress. When change is imposed your life may feel out of control, but you can control the way you respond. Change your attitude – and your language – and you change your life and focus on new opportunities.

The power of positive thought arises from your ability to reframe negative thoughts and to disconnect from your past and think positively about your present and future.

If you refuse to dwell on the negative, your mind creates the positive for you, especially when you give voice to it in positive language.

Treasure Chest

JADE
Traditionally a stone of luck and protection in China, Jade's gentle energy is excellent for reframing negative thoughts and finding inner serenity. This stone encourages becoming who you really are.

RICHTERITE
Although high vibration, Richterite's greatest power lies in assisting the body to withstand constant stress or sudden trauma especially at times of great change. It imparts strength to the physical, mental and subtle bodies helping you to think positively. A profoundly calming stone, it deepens relaxation and meditation, turning off the mind and all anxieties to create a quiet space so that the body switches on its own natural healing mechanisms and rebalances itself.

Try This
Identify your most negative thought (*see page 20*) and find its positive opposite. For the next week, hold this positive thought at least once a day, preferably when you wake up.

Crystal Tips for Positive Thought

Aegirine, Ammolite, Carnelian, Emerald, Flint,
Fulgarite, Howlite, Iron Pyrite, Jade, Magnesite, Ruby.

TOOL 17: GUARDIAN ANGELS

Guardian angels aren't merely vaguely religious figures somewhere 'out there', they are dynamic inner figures here to help you with your life, although they can also manifest through other people and often appear as figures who watch over you. Angels vibrate at a higher frequency than the Earth, which is why crystals are a useful intermediary with them. The more conscious you are of your guardian angel and the more you call on this beautiful being, the more self-protection you'll receive. Invoking an angel is particularly useful if you are walking in a dark place, if you have a difficult task to perform or if you're meeting someone with whom there is a conflict. But, as with everything to do with psychic self-protection, it's no use waiting until you need your angel before you try to make contact, so do it now.

There are several crystals that assist you in making contact with angelic beings. Choose one from the list on page 46 or use a stone you've picked up that speaks of angels to you. You'll often find White Flint in the shape of an angel's wing, but you could also use a white feather to symbolize your guardian angel.

Treasure Chest

CELESTITE

A high-vibration stone, Celestite links to the angelic realms and your guardian angel and stimulates spiritual insights. It brings about profound inner peace, dispersing anxieties, calming incandescent emotions and promoting clarity of mind.

ANGEL'S WING CALCITE

High-vibration Angel's Wing stimulates the soul star, stellar gateway and other higher crown chakras bringing in spiritual light and facilitating angelic contact. Making you feel more comfortable in incarnation, this gentle stone harmonises the brain hemispheres, integrates the lightbody and grounds higher-dimensional energies into the physical plane.

Try This: Meeting the Angel of Protection

- Spend a few moments relaxing, breathing gently and evenly and letting any tension flow out of your body through your hands and feet. Hold your angelic crystal in your hand and place it over your heart.
- When you're ready, picture a shaft of light coming down in front of you and reaching into your heart. This shaft of light reaches from the high-vibration angelic realms down to the earth plane.

Ask your angel to travel down this shaft of light to meet you.

- When your angel arrives, feel it move to stand behind you, wrapping you in protective wings.
- Spend as long as you like with your angel, building up trust and enjoying the sense of protection. Ask your angel whenever you need self-protection. Affirm that this is so.
- Ask the angel to make a powerful connection to your crystal so that whenever you hold the crystal, your angel will be present.
- Thank your angel for being there and let the shaft of light recede back to the angelic realms.
- Before opening your eyes, check that you are enclosed in a bubble of light and that the earth chakra beneath your feet (*see page 105*) is open, grounding you.
- When you are ready, bring your attention fully back into the room and open your eyes.

Crystal Tips for Angelic Contact

Ajoite, Amphibole, Angelite, Angel's Hair (Rutilated Quartz), Angel's Wing Calcite, Aquamarine, Candle Quartz, Celestite, Danburite, Dumortierite, Lemurian Seed Quartz, Morganite, Muscovite, Paraiba Tourmaline, Phantom Quartz, Selenite, Tanzanite, Tugtupite, White Elestial Quartz, White Flint.

TOOL 18: PSYCHIC SHIELDS
....

Psychic shields protect your energy from being intruded or drawn upon by others. The light bubble already mentioned is one form of psychic shield, but there are many others. Basically, because a psychic shield protects your energies, it can be any shape. It can be created right around you, as in the light bubble, but can also be envisaged as a shield you deploy to block negative energy before it reaches you, or in which you can see your 'enemy' reflected. The Greek hero Hercules looked into his shield when he lopped off the Medusa's head, as looking at her directly would have turned him to stone but seeing her in a mirror did not. Traditionally, the Archangel Michael has a sword and shield with which to deal with negative forces.

Treasure Chest

STIBNITE

Metallic silver Stibnite is a toxic stone that must be handled with care (wash your hands after use). It creates an energetic shield around your physical body and protects you during journeying (*see page 53*) and brings you safely home to your physical body. Used with focused intention, it separates the pure from the dross and releases negative energy. It helps you to recognize the gift in difficult experiences and is useful if you need to remove tentacles from clingy relationships, especially after physical separation.

You can create a specific shield that you can turn to any direction to block energy from reaching you simply by programming a crystal. One of the most effective psychic shields in an emergency is to visualize a bright new shiny metal dustbin with a lid, into which you pop when you need extra protection.

Treasure Chest

NUNDERITE

Nunderite is an excellent grounding and shielding stone. It provides a calm, still centre in which to anchor your energies during times of turmoil, change or multi-dimensional journeying. It encourages cooperation and draws like-minded people, moving out of your orbit anyone who is not for your highest good. It facilitates multi-dimensional psychic protection, creating an impenetrable interface around the aura. Effective if you have been under prolonged psychic attack, it cleanses the aura and charges it with light.

Try This

In your mind's eye picture a bright new dustbin of silver metal with a tight-fitting lid. Practise jumping in and out of this dustbin and pulling the lid down so that when you need it, it is an automatic action.

Crystal Tips for a Psychic Shield

*A metallic wand-shaped crystal such as Stibnite makes
an excellent psychic shield (but wash your hands
after use), as do Actinolite, Amber, Aegirine, Apache
Tear, Aquamarine, Black Tourmaline, Bronzite, Citrine
Chlorite, Hematite, Marcasite, Nunderite, Nuummite,
Purpurite, Richterite, Shungite or Smoky Quartz. If you
can find a shield-shaped piece, so much the better.*

TOOL 19: VISION BOARDS

Vision boards are extremely useful reminders of what you
are aiming to manifest. Creating a vision board focuses
your attention and intention and can be a ceremonial task.

To create a board, gather together all the images,
pictures and symbols you can find related to what you
want and stick them onto a large piece of cardboard
around a photograph of yourself.

Try This

Collect together images of things that make you feel
safe and secure. These might be things from your
childhood such as a teddy bear or a particular piece
of clothing, a guardian angel or animal ally picture,
comfort food, a castle – whatever feels good to
you. Arrange them on a board around a photo of
yourself and place it where you will see it often.

TOOL 20: TRADITIONAL SYMBOLS

Sacred geometry, the use of certain shapes to compel
energy to flow in specific ways, is as old as time itself, as is

its use in creating sacred space. Symbols can be inscribed with a pen, chalk, salt or other materials on the floor or a door. They can also be cut into crystals or drawn on stones to provide protection and safe space.

The Pentagram

The pentagram is one such symbol of protection. Older than Wicca and occultism, which adopted it, it is the shape inscribed by the planet Venus during its eight-year journey around the sky and it's believed that Mesopotamian astronomers noted this astronomical pattern over 5,000 years ago. As an Egyptian star symbol, it was believed to bring the favour of the gods down to Earth and to provide their protection. In medieval Christianity it represented the five wounds of Christ and was believed to protect against witches and demons.

Formed from one continuous line, the intersection of the sides follows the 'golden ratio' and symbolizes the spiritual adage 'as above, so below'. A pentagram can be worn, inscribed in the air above your head or placed over an entrance door or around your bed or a chair. Its advantage is that if you want to protect your workplace, you can do so invisibly by drawing a pentagram.

Protective pentagrams are particularly effective when laid out with crystals at each point and at the crossing points. Such pentagrams, even when small, quickly provide protection against ill-wishing and geopathic or electromagnetic stress, as the crystal energy maximizes the radiating power of the symbol. They can provide useful protection when travelling.

A pentagram

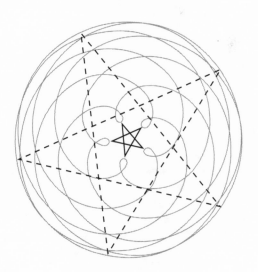

The Venus pentagram

Try This

Before getting into a car, bus, train or plane, mentally draw a pentagram over your head and over the vehicle as a whole.

The Hexagram

The hexagram is another useful protective shape. Constructed from two overlapping triangles, it's often known as the Seal of Solomon or Star of David. Again, although this symbol has been adopted by modern occultism, it's an older symbol going back to biblical times and is used in synagogues and temples.

A symbol of balance, it has one triangle that is positive and one that is negative and is useful for drawing positive energies down to Earth and releasing the negative. A hexagram can, however, also be drawn using a continuous line to create a beautiful star shape with an overlap in the centre that creates a multi-dimensional space through which to access higher levels of consciousness and the angelic realms.

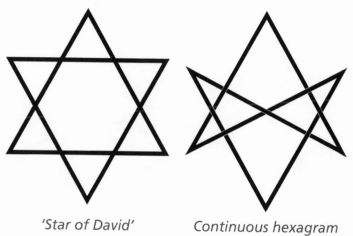

'Star of David'   Continuous hexagram

Try This

Take a small flat pebble and, using a felt-tip pen, draw the protective symbol on it that speaks to you. Keep it in your pocket to protect you.

Crystal Tip

A flat Flint or Milk Quartz pebble is ideal.

TOOL 21: JOURNEYING

Journeying is a form of visioning (*see page 37*) that takes you deep into yourself, into the shamanic underworld to meet power allies or into the celestial upper world to meet angels, your highest Self and guardian beings. It is assisted by music with an insistent beat, such as drumming, and with a distinctive ending, as this calls you back. It is best carried out lying down with your eyes closed in a quiet place where you won't be disturbed. When you're journeying it's more important to *feel* the journey taking place rather than to have pictures of what is happening, although there can be graphic images present. In shamanic journeying a tunnel, cave or tree root is often used to reach the underworld or you may find yourself travelling through the stars. The Guardian Angel and Animal Allies tools (*see pages 44 and 61*) use journeying, and other journeys are found throughout the book. The grounding root (*see page 29*) is a useful start and end to journeying.

Treasure Chest

SHAMAN QUARTZ

Shaman Quartz has many inclusions – layers of material – that form canyons and mountains through which you can journey. It's an excellent stone for breaking family patterns with a compassionate heart and for clearing a build-up of stagnant energy. Healing cellular memory and assisting in getting to the root of problems, Shaman Quartz is a powerful soul healer.

LODOLITE

The inclusions in Lodolite vary greatly and each adds to the effect of the stone. This stone assists journeying to find serenity, peace, insight, communication with higher beings, spiritual growth, exploring your past lives or the multi-dimensions in which your consciousness exists. This gentle loving stone emanates harmony and is a powerful manifestation crystal.

Try This: A Crystal Journey

Hold a Shaman or other Phantom Quartz, Lodolite, Brandenberg, Preseli Bluestone, or any crystal that has distinct planes or inclusions within it.

With your eyes half closed, allow yourself to drift gently into the crystal and follow its inner planes and multi-dimensions. Let the crystal take you where it will.

When it's time to return, withdraw your attention from the crystal, telling yourself firmly you're returning to the present moment and the earth dimension and your physical body. Ground yourself by putting down your root deep into the Earth and standing up and stamping your feet.

Crystal Tips for Journeying

Auralite 23, Banded Agate, Brandenberg or Phantom Quartz, Celestobarite, Elestial Quartz, Green Ridge Quartz, Lodolite, Merlinite, Obsidian, Preseli Bluestone, Rutile, Shaman Quartz, Spirit Quartz.

TOOL 22: SMUDGING

Smudging is yet another ancient tool for space clearing – there are pictures in Egyptian temples of fragrant smoke being wafted to cleanse the space and this is still done today in churches through incense. You can use joss sticks, incense or dried herbs such as sage, artemesia or sweetgrass, or burn frankincense in an oil burner (but never leave an oil burner unattended). It's traditional to use a feather to waft the smoke in the four directions – north, south, east and west – or around a body, but you can gently blow it if you prefer (be careful if blowing near an oil burner, as the candle may flare up). Remember to hold your intention as you waft the smoke around the area.

Try This

Light a joss stick and walk slowly around a room, blowing the smoke gently around the space, paying special attention to the corners, behind the furniture and so on.

Crystal Tip for Cleansing

Sulphur used to be burned as a room cleanser, particularly after illness, but the smoke is quite noxious and it's better simply to place the crystal in the room and ask it to cleanse the energies. (Remember to wash your hands after handling it.) Halite also works well.

TOOL 23: GRATITUDE AND BLESSING

Thanking whoever is working with you, whether they are guides, guardians, angels, allies or your own higher energies, reinforces the process, as do gratitude and appreciation. The more you bless and feel blessed, the more blessed you are.

Treasure Chest

RHODOCHROSITE

A stone of infinite compassion and unconditional love, Rhodochrosite helps you to pinpoint ongoing patterns in which you and others are stuck and to release them and face the truth without judgement. It brings peace into your home or your neighbourhood.

Treasure Chest

BLUE EUCLASE

Euclase is known as the Stone of Happiness and Blue Euclase instils deep peace and inner clarity, a quiet calm centredness that easily copes with change or trauma. It helps you to value your own achievements and true worth. This gentle stone helps you to show gratitude for the riches garnered by your soul and facilitates forgiveness. It takes you deep into the recesses of your own psyche, the shamanic underworld or the furthest reaches of creation. This stone helps you to speak only truth and brings clarity to your mind and your intentions. Grid Blue Euclase to bring deep peace into your home or your neighbourhood.

Try This

Every time you have a positive thought, thank yourself for having that thought.

Crystal Tips for Positive Thought

Blue Euclase, Mangano Calcite, Rhodochrosite, Rose Quartz and Tugtupite help you to express gratitude and blessing.

TOOL 24: BELIEVING IN YOURSELF

You can do it, you have the power within you, you just need to believe it! The more you believe it, the easier it is. Once you have confidence in yourself, everything else follows.

Treasure Chest

MOSS AGATE

Moss Agate is a stone of strength, useful for grounding and for creativity. It encourages trust, assists self-expression and helps in raising self-esteem and strengthening the determination to succeed. It also assists you in getting along with other people and creating your own space.

TREMOLITE

A stone of higher knowledge and connection on many levels, Tremolite draws people to you. Grid Tremolite in disturbed environments to restore peace and tranquillity. Enhancing innate trust, Tremolite offers strength and courage to people struggling with a difficult situation. It eases anxiety or panic wherever it arises and clears emotional baggage, breaking through denial.

Try This

Each time you have a challenge to meet, say to yourself: 'I believe I can do this, I have the power.' Feel that belief in every cell of your body. Believe it!

Crystal Tips for Self-Belief and Confidence
Actinolite, Blue Euclase, Candle Quartz, Cat's Eye Quartz, Citrine, Dumortierite, Empowerite, Eudialyte, Hematite, Lazulite, Purpurite, Pyrite, Rhyolite, Sodalite, Strawberry Quartz, Tree, Moss and other Agates, Strontianite, Tremolite.

TOOL 25: HAPPINESS

Research shows that feeling happy can not only quickly de-stress you but it also makes you healthier and more able to cope with change. It actually creates a physical change within your body – just as eating a piece of scrumptious chocolate feeds your endorphin system.

Treasure Chest

PINK CRACKLE QUARTZ
Pink Crackle Quartz is full of joy and children love it. The underlying strength and energy-enhancing qualities of Quartz are packaged in a way that gently draws out emotional pain and replaces it with love. This stone facilitates the emotional independence that arises from no longer worrying what other people think about you and helps you to follow your own inner guidance rather than being told what to do or how to feel. It shows you how to be responsible for your feelings, recognizing they arise inside yourself and that only you can opt for inner peace rather than relying on other people to provide this.

If you feel happy within yourself, you have a natural equilibrium and the outside world has little effect on you. No matter how abysmal that outside world may be, you can find inner peace by attuning to your inner joy (*see below*).

Treasure Chest

CRINOIDAL LIMESTONE

Crinoidal Limestone was created from primitive echinoderms. As with all fossils, this stone helps you to explore your roots and deep-seated issues, and to find core stability. The stone still retains its essential life-force and represents how our soul is shaped throughout its long journey. Assisting you in moving away from ingrained patterning to follow your own script, it helps to weather changes by creating an interface with the outside world that protects your core stability.

The Inner Smile

The inner smile is an ancient Taoist practice that has been imported into other traditions. It only takes a few moments of your time and has the advantage of being able to be done anywhere without anyone else being aware of it.

Try This

- Smile widely and remember a time that made you smile or laugh out loud. Remember the time when you were happiest of all. Feel how joy

floods through your body and your heart lifts.
Feel how good that is.

- Now take that happiness slowly down through
  your body, starting at the top of your head and
  working your way down. It can help to picture
  one of those smiley faces people use at the end
  of e-mails.
- With a little practice, you can send an instant
  smile to any part of your body that feels unhappy
  or dis-eased and rapidly bring joyful ease.

Crystal Tip for Happiness

Hold a Pink Crackle Quartz, Blue Euclase, Crinoidal
Limestone, Eudialyte, Rose Quartz or Tugtupite for instant joy.

TOOL 26: ANIMAL ALLIES

Shamanic cultures the world over use animal allies for
protection and guidance.[4] Calling on an animal ally means
you'll always feel safe.

Useful Allies

Here's a list of some animal allies and the qualities and
strengths they bring:

- *Bear:* Nurturing and primal power, defending your
  boundaries.
- *Bee:* Banding together, seeing the spirits of the dead.
- *Buzzard/Falcon:* Intuitive perception and the
  far-sighted view.
- *Cat:* The ability to shape-shift and move unseen,
  independence.

- *Cougar/Jaguar/Panther:* The power of invisibility and protection, especially against control freaks who want to run your life or those who sneak up unseen. The ability to rise above events.
- *Coyote:* The ability to laugh at yourself and your follies, wiliness, learning the lesson and the wisdom in the everyday.
- *Deer:* Gentleness, trusting your intuition, giving up trying to figure things out with your head, gratitude.
- *Dog:* Guardian of the gateway to the underworld, loyalty and companionship.
- *Dolphin:* Playful wisdom and spontaneous play, communication, recouping your strength, rhythm and flow.
- *Lion:* Courage and the ability to defend your family.
- *Raven:* Protection against ill-wishing, assists initiation.
- *Snake:* Transformation, core energy, healing power, sexuality, rebirth.
- *Spider:* Weaving the web of fate, creativity, seeing through the web of illusion.
- *Tiger:* Power, strength in the face of adversity, acting in a timely manner, action without analysis.
- *Turtle:* Centredness, psychic protection, respect for others, the ability to navigate skilfully, patience.
- *Whale:* Creation, soulmaking and soul path, following the flow, being a record keeper, having psychic abilities.
- *Wolf:* Spirit guardian, protection against attack on the unseen levels, cunning, learning, shadow energy, spirit teaching, death and rebirth, outwitting enemies, loyalty.

Treasure Chest

LARIMAR
Ethereal Larimar opens you to new dimensions by dissolving spurious boundaries and limitations. Removing self-imposed restraints and blockages, it dissolves self-sabotaging behaviour and helps you to take control of your life. If you've a tendency towards guilt or fear, this stone replaces it with serenity. It's an excellent stone for 'going with the flow' and calls in dolphin energy.

BUMBLE BEE JASPER
This vibrant stone helps you to achieve the impossible and brings great joy into your life. It enhances trust and reminds you that are a divine being with immense inner riches.

Calling your Animal Ally
The following journey is best done to music. A drumbeat is ideal. Always ensure the music has a definite end to call you back, and do the journey at a time when you will be undisturbed. Remember to record the experience in your journal.

Try This: Calling your Animal Ally
- Lie down comfortably and cover yourself with a blanket. If you have an animal ally crystal, hold it in your hand.

- Close your eyes and breathe gently, withdrawing your attention from the outside world and focusing it on your third eye.
- Now picture yourself standing on the seashore with an island close by. In front of you there is a boat with a boatman waiting to row you across to the island. Settle yourself comfortably in the boat and as you approach the island ask that your animal ally be there to meet you.
- Notice who comes to greet you as the boat is tied up. Take time to get to know your animal ally. If you explore the island, you may find further allies waiting for you.
- When you return to the boat, ask that the allies may accompany you back to the mainland and be available to you when you need them.
- When the boat returns to the beach, thank the boatman and step out onto the beach with your animal allies. Thank them and ask them to be with you and to keep you safe.
- When you open your eyes, close down and ground yourself by stamping your foot firmly on the Earth.
- Whenever you have to walk in dark places or feel vulnerable, call on your animal ally or allies to be present and to protect you.

Crystal Tips for Animal Allies

Bumble Bee Jasper calls in bee helpers, Celestobarite carries coyote energy; Larimar, that of the dolphin and the Earth Mother; Leopardskin Jasper, Agate or Serpentine, jaguar, leopard, cougar or panther energy;

Snakeskin Agate calls in serpent helpers; Stibnite, wolf energy and Tree Agate connects to insect allies.

TOOL 27: CRYSTAL EFT

Crystal EFT is a variation of the Emotional Freedom Technique,[5] which uses specific 'tapping points' on the energetic meridians of your body to identify and clear negative emotions, toxic thoughts and destructive behaviour patterns and to instil confidence if you're faced with a challenge. Tapping with a crystal point, particularly that of an Amethyst, Brandenberg or Smoky Quartz, dramatically heightens the transformation, as the crystal absorbs and transmutes the negativity that is released during the tapping, so remember to cleanse it thoroughly after each use and, if it feels right, between each round of tapping. However, you don't need to use a crystal to gain benefit from tapping, you can simply use your fingers. (*See page 130 for full instructions on how to tap and the tapping points.*) Remember to tap with focused intention.

Try This: Calling your Spirit Home

- Using all your fingertips, tap the points either side of your breastbone about a hand's breadth below the collarbone (which are known as 'spirit ground' in Chinese medicine). Tapping these points eases the pain of being in incarnation and also helps with emotional pain. It calls your spirit home to your physical body and is useful in releasing any spiritual, mental or emotional pain.

- As you tap, say out loud: 'I deeply and profoundly love, accept and forgive myself unconditionally and completely as I call my spirit home.'

And see Believing in Yourself **(Tool 23, page 58)**.

And finally

Now that you have established the tools that resonate with you, practise applying them in different situations to see which work best for you. The next section has many examples of where these tools can be used to bring you lasting inner peace and enable you to face change with equanimity.

Treasure Chest

GREEN RIDGE QUARTZ

Green Ridge Quartz is one of the most powerful new healing crystals with exceptionally high vibrations. Green Ridge is found in Clear, Amethyst, Orange, Golden and Iron-coated forms (see page 235). The different forms are a continuum of healing energy and are perfect for laying on the chakras to cleanse and purify them and especially for activating the higher chakras. The combination disassembles everything that's happened previously so that a new programme can go in, and then clarifies and fine-tunes the energies.

PART II
ELIMINATE THE NEGATIVE

Eliminate the Negative

'You may be rejected, locked up, spat on, pushed around, lied about and so on, but inside you are unwavering in your self-regard and self-knowledge of who you really are. That is a truly powerful place to live from.'

Leo Rutherford, 'The View From the Medicine Wheel' in *Watkins Review*, Spring 2009

As we've seen, negative thoughts and emotions, environmental pollution and so on can create a subtle feeling of unrest, agitation and anxiety, what I call 'dis-ease'. If unchecked, this subtle dis-ease can lead to more serious conditions, both physically and emotionally. In this part of the book we will look at further ways to clear ourselves of negativity, internal and external, and will discover how to remove the attractors that might be pulling detrimental energy and people towards us.

We will be working on the subtle bodies as well as our mental and emotional state. These subtle bodies are contained within the aura and are linked to the physical body by the chakras, centres which mediate and distribute energy throughout the physical and subtle bodies as required. The chakras can themselves become blocked and need regular cleansing and re-energizing. We will look at various ways of toning them up and re-energizing them.

Just as you have a physical immune system, so too you have a psychic immune system. These two systems are the front line of defence against dis-ease. If they are not functioning well, dis-ease and organisms – physical or psychic, or energy leeches and noxious energies – can invade, so we will also be looking at how to revitalize them.

Your need for psychic self-protection is perhaps at its strongest when you are out and about: travelling, shopping, working or just having fun, but it is essential to love and work in a safe space. You can wear a crystal to keep yourself safe, wrap yourself in a light bubble in a crowd, put a pentagram symbol over your mode of transport and check out the energies wherever you go. You might also like to think about the space when you move house, cleansing both the one left behind and the one into which you move.

CREATING SAFE SPACES

Making sure that the space around you is safe and secure is one of the most important aspects of self-protection after securing your inner space. There are various space invaders, with other people's energies or emotions, electromagnetic emanations or geopathic stress being the major factors.

Electromagnetic pollution arises from computers, mobile phone masts and the like. If you suddenly find you're not sleeping, for example, check whether a new mast has gone up and grid your space with suitable crystals. Geopathic stress arises from ley lines, underground water and so on, and again can be diverted by suitably placed crystals. Amazonite, Black Tourmaline, Herkimer Diamond, Quantum Quattro, Shungite or Smoky Quartz will protect you against such stress (remember to cleanse them regularly) and gridding around your house or workplace with these crystals usually affords excellent protection, but if the stress is particularly strong, you may need to call in an experienced dowser to check the property and divert the lines.

The energy that you, your family, friends and strangers bring into your home, leisure or workspace or when you're travelling, for example, also needs cleansing. Too much fear or anger, too many pessimistic thoughts, or envy, jealousy and similar negative emotions can generate a toxic soup. So, the first step is to cleanse your space and to protect it.

SPACE CLEARING

Your own strong emotions, hopes or fears, other people's emanations and the events of the day can energetically 'pollute' your home or workplace. Even the programmes you watch on television can change the vibrations for better or worse, as do the attitudes of your co-workers. Space pollution can also come about through deliberate targeting or simply from a spirit who has passed on but forgotten to depart. Space clearing is also useful if you share space used by other people or you have to enter a new space – I always take Clear2Light, a Petaltone space-clearing essence (*see Essences, page 18, and Resources*), in a spray with me when I travel, for instance, so I can ensure that I sleep in an energetically clean bedroom, and it's essential for me to clean the space and protect the room I am working in with crystals and a golden pyramid before starting a talk or a workshop. Crystal Cleanser also clears space.

While in no way engendering fear or anxiety about it, scheduling regular space clearing is essential, say once a week, as is being alert to subtle changes in atmosphere – if you suddenly feel overwhelming tiredness or anger it can be a sign that some space clearing is needed.

Try This

As you step through your front door, consciously monitor the energies in the house. Notice if your energy rises or drops, or if you suddenly become tired or shiver or begin to feel vaguely unwell after you've been in the house for a short time. If you do, have a Halite shower (*see page 128*) in case you've picked up any adverse energy on your way home and check the energy again. (You may also need to grid the house, *see page 14*).

On Stand-by?

Quite apart from being bad for the environment on account of the excess energy consumed, leaving electrical items such as computers, mobile phones or televisions on stand-by is counterproductive to an energetically safe home, as they fill the house with negative electromagnetic energy. If you must leave a computer on, have a negative ionizer running at the same time and place a large anti-electromagnetic pollution crystal close by and cleanse it often. Keep an Amazonite, Black Tourmaline or Shungite crystal taped to a mobile phone, even a low-emissions one.[6]

Treasure Chest

SHUNGITE

With what is possibly the most phenomenal shielding power of all the crystals, Shungite strengthens your energetic boundaries and protects you against geopathogens, electromagnetic frequencies, geopathic stress and invaders such as viruses and bacteria. It clears out mental or emotional pollutants so that fresh patterns imprint, and boosts physical well-being which has a powerful effect on the immune system. Restoring emotional equilibrium, it transmutes stress into a potent energetic recharge.

Treasure Chest

AMAZONITE

An excellent protection against geopathic and electromagnetic emanations of all kinds, Amazonite has a strong filtering action on the physical and mental levels. A soothing stone for emotional or physical trauma, it alleviates worry and assists in seeing both points of view.

Crystal Tips against Electromagnetic Stress

Amazonite, Fluorite, Lepidolite, Quantum Quattro, Shungite or Smoky Quartz placed on or near electrical items, Black Tourmaline or Shungite taped to your mobile phone.

Crystal Tips against Geopathic Stress

Amazonite, Black Tourmaline, Diamond, Elestial Quartz, Herkimer Diamond, Jasper, Kunzite, Quantum Quattro, Shungite or Smoky Quartz - grid around the house or on the lines.

Additional Tools

Crystal Layouts (*Tool 2, page 14*), Smudging (*Tool 22, page 55*).

Space Invasion

Space invasion occurs when an energy that isn't conducive to your well-being or emotional equilibrium enters or is left behind in your space. You can easily tell if it has happened, as one and probably more of these symptoms will be present:

- insomnia or panic attacks
- excessive yawning or a choking cough
- constant small infections and colds
- unpleasant or unusual smells
- cold patches
- feeling vaguely out of sorts and ill at ease
- formerly clear crystals look murky
- a child or animal is disturbed
- light bulbs blow frequently
- electrical apparatus malfunctions
- the energy feels like walking through treacle.

Of course, if you've already strengthened your auric boundaries, you won't be as badly affected, but nevertheless regular energetic house cleaning is essential if you're to live safely and be well protected.

Your first line of defence against space invasion, and the way to maintain a safe space thereafter, is to cleanse the energies thoroughly, for which there are several tools available (*see below*).

'Out of my Space!'

Something may need banishing from your space, such as an energy imprint someone has left behind. It may be someone living who is showing undue interest in what is going on there or someone who refuses to move out even though they've passed on. It may be someone who has lived or worked in the space with you, such as a former partner, who now needs moving out, or it may be someone from the spirit world who is stuck. (Spirit rescue work usually needs professional handling, but there are emergency measures you can take, *see page 122*). It can also be someone who is living in your space legitimately but who is putting out strongly negative vibes – in which case you first need to decide whether you want to go on living within their energy field and what you'll do about it if you don't, or to find a way to discuss neutralizing it if you want to go on living together.

The following exercise uses the most basic stones there are – pebbles picked up from your immediate surroundings. Flint pebbles are particularly good for this exercise, as they readily absorb and hold energy. As with all exercises, this one is immeasurably more effective when carried out with strong intention.

Try This

For each room to be cleared you will need four pebbles. Flint is particularly effective for this exercise.

- Hold the pebbles in your hand and dedicate them to clearing your space of this particular energy imprint. Say whatever words come to mind such as 'Out of my space', 'Be gone', 'It's time to leave' or whatever is appropriate.

- Now place a pebble at each corner of the room (if the room is still occupied by the person, you may need to position the pebbles under furniture where they won't be noticed and cannot be moved). In your mind's eye, see them connected by a shining grid of light or connect them up with a crystal wand. Leave them in place for one week.

Adding Petaltone Astral Clear or Special 8 can strengthen the effect (*see Resources*).

- After a week, gather them up and throw them entirely out of your space – into a stream, river or the sea is ideal, but a puddle at the side of the road does at a push. As you do so, say out loud: 'Be gone from my space and stay out.' If you can send forgiveness and unconditional love with the stones, so much the better.

- Go back into the room and say out loud: 'I reclaim my space.' Smudge or spray with a cleansing spray such as Green Man Earthlight, Living Tree Soul Shield or Petaltone Clear2Light and, where possible, grid each corner of the room with Selenite to restore the light. Mentally fill the room with pink light, love, forgiveness and a big smile.

The 'Kick-Ass' Combination

If someone is in your space and you don't want them to be – guests who have stayed too long or an ex-partner who won't move out, for example – you could try the 'kick-ass crystal' combination, so called because these crystals have proved to be so effective in getting people out – fast. Friends of mine had, uninvited, visitors from Australia who turned up and announced they had a return ticket for six months' time. They ate my friends' food, used all their facilities, monopolized their TV, didn't offer to pay anything, drove – and damaged – their car, and hung around whenever people called. Although my friends are generous people, after three months it was a nightmare scenario. I took over the kick-ass crystals, suitably programmed to help them get their space back, and we placed them on a table in the hall. Within a week the visitors announced they'd changed their flight and were off home.

The crystal combination involves quite a rare stone, Red Feldspar with Phenacite, but you could use any red stone such as Red Jasper or Carnelian, together with a more easily obtained stone, Smoky Quartz. The particular Smoky Quartz I use looks like a hand pointing out the exit and the Red Feldspar with Phenacite looks like a boot. Another of my friends used the same crystals to persuade an ex-boyfriend to finally move out almost three months after the relationship had finished. She placed the boot-shaped stone at the foot of his sleeping bag (yes, he really did keep his sleeping bag rolled up and stashed behind the couch) and the 'way out' sign went into the hall. He was gone in a couple of days.

In both cases no animosity accompanied the use of the crystals; they were programmed with the intention that the people would go of their own accord to something better, which was what happened. The ex-boyfriend found a flat and the couple went home for the birth of a grandchild. The combination had an unexpected benefit for my friend, too, as she met the love of her life and is now happier than she has ever been.

SPACE-CLEARING TOOLS

The following tools work well whether for simple space clearing of murky energies or for more in-depth cleansing such as clearing the energies left behind when someone moves or as the result of ill-wishing (*see page 178*). The effectiveness of all the space-clearing tools is heightened when they are used with intention.

Smudging

Purpose-made smudge sticks (*see Tool 22, page 55*) are available in many outlets, but you can make your own from dried sage, sweetgrass or artemesia sprigs bound tightly together with wool or string, or burn frankincense resin or essential oil to cleanse your space.

Try This: Using a Smudge Stick

- Light the smudge stick (or joss, incense or frankincense) until it is smoking well.
- Face each of the four directions – north, south, east and west – in turn, and either gently blow smoke into them or guide it there with a feather.
- Let the smoke fill the whole room, paying special attention to the corners and behind furniture.
- To extinguish the smudge stick, place it in a tin and put the lid on.

Sound

Sound is both an excellent way to check out whether there are any negative energies around and a particularly effective – and rapid – way to cleanse space.

Try This

- Clap your hands loudly. If the sound is flat and lifeless, the space needs clearing. If the sound rings out true and clear, your space is clear.
- Clap all around the house, paying particular attention to 'dead' areas in the corner or behind furniture.

Cymbals or tingshas, drums, gongs, Tibetan bowls and other instruments such as the voice can also be used for space clearing. Walk around the room slowly, again paying particular attention to the corners and to the quality of the sound. A chanting or drumming CD quickly revives energies, but you can use music of any kind so long as it feels good to you.

Treasure Chest

HEMATITE

An ancient grounding and protection stone, Hematite prevents negative energies from entering the aura, It strengthens willpower and intention and draws your attention to outdated programmes, transmuting them.

SPACE-CLEARING ESSENCES

There are some excellent space-clearing essences available from health stores or via the internet (*see Resources*) or you can make your own (*see Tool 5 page 18*). Essences are made by immersing flowers, trees or crystals in water, often with oils and alcohol to preserve them. The Petaltone Clear2Light (formerly Crystal Clear), and Z14 (etheric levels) essences have been specially formulated to protect your energies and clean the space around you, as have other space-clearing essences such as the excellent Living Tree Orchid Essence Soul Shield, Bush Space Clearing and the Alaskan, Green Man and Crystal Balance essences sprays. Petaltone also make the extremely useful Astral Clear and Special 8 essence for moving on stuck spirits – those departed, and often bewildered, souls who have become trapped in a room they once knew. These space-clearing essences are extremely powerful in their own right, but your focused intention nevertheless boosts their innate energy.

Space-clearing essences can be used in three basic ways:

1. For personal clearing, if the essence is not already in a spray bottle, place a few drops of it in the palms of your hands and disperse it around your body about a hand's breadth out from your skin, or spray it from a misting bottle. Remember to do both your front and back. This protects your aura and prevents you from absorbing energies from the environment or from other people. It should be used when you feel tired or drained, as it clears energies you've inadvertently picked up.

2. For space clearing, spray the room or put a few drops of the essence on a crystal and place in your pocket or near your bed, desk or meditation place.

3. For personal or space clearing, if the essence is not already in a spray bottle, place three or four drops in a mister or spray and top it up with water. Either spray this around yourself to clean your energies of anything negative you may have picked up, or spray the space around you. This is particularly useful for working spaces, hotel rooms or bedrooms and it's beneficial when travelling, especially on crowded planes or other public transport. (Do not take internally). If you are spraying a room, remember to do all the corners and behind furniture.

Petaltone Astral Clear or Special 8 is used slightly differently, as it works best when placed on a Quartz crystal and left to clear the room and send a stuck spirit to the light (which is part of its purpose). As you place the crystal, hold the intention that the spirit will find the help and healing that it needs.

Z14 is dropped onto the floor or an Amphibole Quartz or Selenite at your feet, while at the same time invoking the assistance of Archangel Michael. Crystals soaked in Z14 can also be left in a room to keep the energies clear for several months.

Note: A spray bottle of Clear2Light, when left standing in a room, quickly absorbs negative energies and may smell 'musty' when sprayed. If this happens, empty the contents away and boil the spray bottle before refilling.

ACCUMULATED PSYCHIC PROTECTION

David Eastoe, creator of Clear2Light, Z14 and Astral Clear, made his essences to deal with that he calls 'accumulated psychic pollution'. I personally never move far without David's essences; they are absolutely essential to my psychic and crystal work and I always have a bottle in my handbag, to the amusement of friends – many of whom have benefited from the essence in times of need.

I find that, once a room has been cleared, it can be useful to place a crystal imbued with the essence in an unobtrusive place. I used this technique to clear an old house which was used as a workshop centre and which had a particularly nasty 'black energy spot' in one of the rooms. Each time I went there, the negative energies had built up again, despite earlier clearing. As it happened, David Eastoe came to one of my workshops to demonstrate his new Z14 essence, which definitely helped with the build-up of old energies, but it didn't hold beyond a month, as I found when I returned. But what did work was repeating the Z14 essence, dripped on Amphibole (Angel) Quartz, in one of his singing bowls on the floor and then placing a Selenite crystal imbued with Clear2Light and Z14 in the (disused) fireplace. That held until I returned again the following year. If David's essences had not cleared that black energy spot, visitors to the centre could well have picked up the angry and negative energies around it. This could have manifested as faintness or coldness, or sudden disagreements. Not everyone would have recognized it was the energy of the room that was making them feel ill or angry. But everyone on my group noticed the difference when the spot had been cleared.

It is possible to be badly affected by the energies on the site of an old battle, even when it's unknown as a battlefield, or the site of similar trauma. Sometimes the feelings picked up psychically masquerade as something entirely *other.* Indeed, there are people who have visited such sites and tuned in to entities still there, or simply the energies of the place, and reported past lives based on what they have picked up (which isn't to say people haven't been reminded of a genuine past life at such spots). Visitors have been haunted by nightmares of the battle, or carried away the psychic energy of the place, leading to a depression that was most probably not even recognized as linking to that visit. The same thing happens at old grave sites and wherever there have been ancient dramas or traumas that have left a psychic residue behind.

For sensitive people, standing on a ley line or place where geopathic stress is strong brings about similar symptoms. For this reason, it's always worth checking the earth energies before meditating or 'working' at a sacred site. Such sites hold the energy imprint of all that has gone before and you cannot assume it was all good – see my earlier example about the energies at Glastonbury.

It is also wise to bear in mind that some people may not want to have the energy around them cleared. People can actually be attached to their negativity and to uninvited guests. I find that if someone is carrying something negative with them, they can have a strong reaction when I spray. I once went to the London Book Fair to meet a publisher. The energy at Olympia was thick and turgid, and there were hundreds of people there. Feeling unable to breathe, I sprayed Clear2Light liberally around myself.

As it landed on the publisher, he jumped violently and shrieked, rubbing at himself as though scalded. I thought this rather strange, as the rest of the people on the stand were commenting on how much better the atmosphere felt, but I paid it no further attention. Some time later, I was on the receiving end of a particularly nasty phone attack from that same publisher – an attack which left a foetid odour hovering around the corner of the room where the phone was, like extremely stale socks. Ti essence on the phone sorted that and I placed a piece of Black Obsidian there to soak up any negative vibes and had no more trouble. But when I recalled the incident with the Clear2Light, someone commented it must have been like applying garlic to a vampire!

I always spray Clear2Light in my workspace or in workshops, or as a completion to readings, past-life or crystal work that releases negative emotions or energies. I also use it after we have done tie-cutting of any kind. It clears the air miraculously. People often ask to be sprayed all over, as they can feel the change of energy instantaneously. Nevertheless, I've noticed that a few people still find the use of Clear2Light unpleasant. These people usually have more work to do, which can include soul retrieval, detaching an entity from their aura, or lifting a curse or vow that has been placed on them. But, as David Eastoe says, it can also indicate someone who is more comfortable remaining the way they are and I've learned I must respect that.

Try This

You can make a space- or crystal-clearing essence by soaking a Black Tourmaline, a piece of clear Quartz and a few grains of frankincense in spring water in the sun for several hours. Add five drops of rosemary or lavender pure essential oil. If the essence is to be kept for more than a day, add one-quarter vodka or 12 drops of glycerine to the spray bottle as a preservative. (Do not take internally.)

CREATING SAFE SPACE

The golden pyramid (*Tool 8, see page 23*) can be adapted to cleanse, energize and protect your space. It only takes a few moments to picture putting the pyramid in place around a building and light filling a room and transmuting the energies into positive ones. You can also use cleansed and dedicated crystals, smudge with sage, or spray with protective essences. If, in an emergency, there are no other tools available, you can use the focused intention of your own mind to purify and protect the space by visualizing symbols or shapes such as the pyramid

Crystals for Safe Space

Crystals are particularly effective for neutralizing the subtle physical and energetic dis-ease and electromagnetic disturbances created by televisions, computers, phones, power lines and such like. A crystal placed outside the house will deflect such negative energies from reaching you at all. Place the point facing away from your space and cleanse it frequently. Inside the house or your workplace, a large Smoky or Elestial Quartz in the hallway, placed point-out, will repel such energies and a large crystal sphere moves on stagnant energies. Remember to regularly cleanse the crystals used to create safe space.

Specific crystals work well for particular needs. Blue, Brown or White Aragonites are powerful earth healers that can be gridded around your house to keep the environment healthy and the neighbourhood vibes good. Brown Aragonites often look like little sputniks. A beautiful Pink Aragonite sphere radiates joy, love and serenity into your home. Atlantasite can be buried in the earth wherever there has been death and destruction on the land, as it clears and restructures the Earth's energy field, filling it with positive energy.

However, it's wise to remember the rule 'like attracts like' when working to create safe space. It's no good creating a safe space for yourself if your motives, emotions and behaviour (or those of anyone else who shares the space) are not in alignment with your stated intention. Say you want to lay out a grid to protect against petty theft. You choose Sardonyx and lay out your grid, but the pilfering continues. You need to ask yourself in your journal (*see Tool 6, page 19*), 'Where in my life am I not scrupulously honest?' You may find you don't always pay meticulous attention to your own integrity, or you're not honest about your emotional feelings or reactions to other people. You may cheat the taxman or fail to pay your bills on time. You may steal time from people or indulge in some petty pilfering yourself if given the opportunity. If so, the grid won't work.

Similarly, if you live with an irritable or pessimistic person or someone who is not scrupulously honest, you cannot keep that energy out of your space. Everything has to be in perfect alignment if safe space is to work for you. The same applies if you take anger into your space, especially if you project it or displace it onto other people rather than dealing with it at source. You cannot protect your space from your own negativity or that of anyone who shares that space, you must clear it from yourself first and then your space.

Bear in mind too that 'as you think, so you are'. Think positively, think clean safe space and you'll create it. I always know when I'm getting angry or frustrated because my computer crashes or a light bulb blows. Staying calm means staying safe.

Try This
A large Chlorite Quartz hung point-down in the lavatory cistern absorbs negative energy from your house and transmutes it with each flush.

Crystals Tips to Prevent Crime
Kyanite, Sardonyx, Selenite. (Grid around the outside of the house or the corners of a room.)

Crystal Tips for Environmental Pollution
- *Amazonite, Black Tourmaline and Shungite block radar/mobile phone mast emanations.*
- *A Black Tourmaline rod in Quartz, Smoky Quartz, Super 7 or Tourmalinated Quartz guards against terrorist attack or can be used to heal the effects of violence or trauma.*
- *Malachite is particularly efficient at soaking up nuclear radiation.*

- *Smoky Quartz and Shungite are excellent for blocking electromagnetic smog of any kind.*
- *Turquoise is an all-round environmental healer and cleanser.*

Crystal Tips for Space Invasion
Black Tourmaline, large Elestial or Smoky Quartz points, large Quartz cluster, Rose Quartz, Selenite, Shungite. (Place at the corners of the room or grid in a pentacle or hexagram, *see pages 50–52.*)

Additional Tools
Positive Thought (*Tool 16, page 42*), Believing in Yourself (*Tool 24, page 58*).

Gridding for Safe Space
Gridding is placing crystals in a specific pattern in your environment to move energy in a certain way or to cleanse and purify it. All stones laid in grids should be cleansed and dedicated before use, but remember to allow the crystals to do what they do best rather than what you feel they should be doing.

When gridding crystals in your environment or around yourself to enhance and contain energies, you can use traditional patterns such as a pentagram or hexagram (*see Tool 2, page 14*), a zig-zag or a figure of eight. Each moves the energy in a different way.

Try This

To protect the energies of a house or room, place an appropriate crystal in each corner. If you have a garden, place the crystals at the outermost corners. Remember to cleanse and dedicate the crystals before use and to cleanse them regularly afterwards (*see Tool 1, page 6*).

The Pentagram

The pentagram is excellent for rebalancing and containing your energetic field and for creating safe living space, but the effect varies according to the crystals used. Experiment with different crystals to see the effects they have, and remember they may need changing over time.

Try This: The Safe Space Pentagram

- Choose 10 tumble stones (see *page 92*) or use pebbles that particularly appeal to you. Your crystals can be all the same type or a mixture, whichever your intuition tells you is best.
- Having cleansed your stones, hold them in your hands for a few moments and ask them to work with you to create a safe space.
- Now lay a stone at the top point of the pentagram and three more stones evenly spaced down to the bottom right-hand point of the pentagram (*see page 51*).
- Lay three more evenly spaced stones going up to the top left-hand point of the pentagram.
- Lay a stone at the first intersection and out at the point of the top right-hand point (you'll already

have a stone laid at the intersection of the first line you laid).

- Now lay a stone at the bottom left-hand point and take your hand back up to the top point to complete the pentagram.

The Figure of Eight

A figure of eight grounds and balances spiritual and earth energies into your body or into your space to help you feel positive. It draws spiritual energy down and melds it with earth energy to create perfect balance. This layout can be left for several weeks to create safe space.

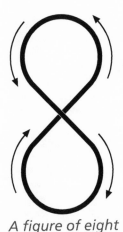

A figure of eight

- Following the direction of the arrows on the diagram, place high-vibration stones such as Amphibole, Brandenberg Amethyst, Danburite, Kunzite, Selenite, Spirit Quartz or Super 7 on points in the top half.
- Then place brown and red grounding stones such as Red Jasper and Smoky Quartz in the lower half.

- Remember to complete the circuit back to the first stone placed.

Crystal Tips for Gridding for Safe Space

- Amethyst: *Protects, draws in spiritual energy and encourages relaxation.*
- Aragonite: *Earth healing.*
- Atlantasite: *Heals the site of trauma or death.*
- Aventurine: *Protects against electromagnetic smog or geopathic stress.*
- Black Tourmaline: *Protects, turns back ill-wishing and crime.*
- Bloodstone: *An immune system stimulator.*
- Blue Chalcedony: *Protects during political unrest.*
- Chlorite: *Cleanses energy and repels disembodied spirits.*
- Dendritic Agate: *An earth healer and crop enhancer.*
- Eye of the Storm: *creates a calm safe haven.*
- Labradorite: *Raises the vibrations and protects (can be used in large raw chunks).*
- Malachite: *Protects against radiation.*
- Sardonyx: *Prevents crime.*
- Selenite: *Raises the vibrations, draws in spiritual light.*
- Smithsonite: *Promotes self-healing.*
- Shungite: *draws off electromagnetic pollution and geopathogens and transmutes negative energy.*
- Super 7: *Calms racial unrest and heals the Earth.*
- Tree Agate: *An earth healer and shamanic protector.*

CRYSTALS TO ENHANCE YOUR WORKSPACE

Crystals are discreet tools for enhancing your workspace and for encouraging cooperation between co-workers. You can use a crystal as a paperweight, slip one into a plant pot or place one on your computer. A small crystal can have just as powerful an effect as a large one. A small Orange Carnelian, for instance, energizes a whole room and a Spirit Quartz brings in cooperation and harmony.

It's also beneficial to spritz the area with suitable gem essences:

Crystal Tips for the workspace

- <u>Blue Lace Agate:</u> *If there is discord within your working environment, Blue Lace Agate quickly restores peace and harmony.*
- <u>Green Aventurine:</u> *Highly effective for absorbing electromagnetic smog and environmental pollution and for creating prosperity, Green Aventurine also promotes empathetic leadership. This crystal defuses negative situations and turns them around. Place one at each corner of your desk, or in the drawers, if you have a co-worker who leaches your energy.*
- <u>Labradorite:</u> *The iridescent energy of Labradorite enhances group energy and improves cooperation. It encourages the acceptance of new ideas and the sharing of insights, which benefits the whole and creates a harmonious working environment.*
- <u>Orange Carnelian:</u> *The vibrant energies of Orange Carnelian keep your workspace as energetic as possible, not in a frenetic way, but rather in a manner which*

optimizes effort. This stone attracts abundant good fortune into your working life, helping you achieve maximum success and getting things done as quickly as possible.

- Shungite: soaks up electromagnetic pollution in the workplace and is particularly useful in a computer- or phone-heavy environment.
- Smoky Quartz: Protecting against other people's stress and frustration as well as blocking electromagnetic smog and geopathic stress, a Smoky Quartz quickly clears your workspace of negative vibes. This stone alleviates communication difficulties – keep one near your telephone and spray the room regularly to clear negativity.
- Sodalite: If your workspace suffers from 'sick building syndrome', Sodalite essence sprayed around the building or placed in the four corners of your room neutralizes the effect. Sick building syndrome is often linked to an hermetically sealed building that has no natural light or air and that suffers from electromagnetic pollution and static electricity. Sodalite also absorbs the emanations of fluorescent tubes and computers. This stone enhances the workings of a group, instilling a sense of trust and solidarity of purpose. It promotes good companionship and harmony between co-workers and its ability to bring things into the open non-judgementally is useful if any kind of assessment or appraisal has to be carried out.
- Spirit Quartz: ensures that the whole working environment is harmonious and that everyone works as a cooperative team for the good of the whole.

CREATING SACRED SPACE: SETTING UP AN ALTAR

Altars have traditionally been used with a religious figure or icon and offerings to delineate a sacred or protected space, but even in a secular society they can be created to mark significant places or events, or to create harmonious relationships. Spontaneous altars often arise these days at places where the death of a public figure or victim has occurred. Alternatively, a shrine may be set up within a room. Such places carry an inherent power that you can harness to create and maintain a sacred space within your home. They also make an ideal focus for visioning or contemplation.

You can use altars for various purposes. Setting up an 'ancestor altar' helps you to honour and remember all the gifts you've received through your family line. This is a particularly powerful altar to set up when you feel badly let down by your family and need to practise forgiveness and gratitude (*see Tool 23, page 56*), as it can help you to find the blessing in your experience.

An altar does not have to be elaborate or showy to be effective. It can be on a shelf or table with just a few treasured items and fresh flowers. My electricity meter is above the stairs and used to face me every time I walked downstairs. I put up a shelf above it, stapled a Tibetan tankhga painting of female deities to it to cover the meters and placed some Spirit Quartz, Serpentine Quan Ying and Green Tara statues on it, and now every time I walk downstairs I honour the feminine divine principle – more pleasing to the eye and the soul than the god of electricity!

Your altar does not need to be indoors either. I also

have a corner of the garden where a Buddha quietly contemplates a bowl of flowers and where a full-moon candle is lit each month. I place cleansed and dedicated crystals on the Buddha to be charged up in the light of the sun and moon. This transforms the whole garden into a sacred space.

Try This: Setting Up an Altar for Sacred Space

- If you've a religious affiliation you can use an associated symbol or figure as the centre of your altar. Otherwise a candle, crystal (a large Elestial Quartz or Selenite tower makes it special), a photograph of a loved one or some other object that has personal meaning to you – even a plant – can become sacred when it is imbued with intent.

- Choose a space that won't be infringed upon by other activities. A small shelf or table is ideal. You can cover it with a special cloth. Silk or velvet is best.

- Place the figure in the centre of the altar and surround it with suitable 'offerings'. Some cultures use oranges or wheat, for instance. The ancient Egyptians used beer. Other people like to use flowers, photographs, crystals, joss sticks and tealights.

- When the altar is complete, contemplate it for a few moments and dedicate it to the highest good of those who live within its sphere. State that it makes the space around it sacred and peaceful. If you've a specific purpose for it, state that out loud.

- Remember to smudge, spray, sound-cleanse or otherwise purify your altar regularly.

HEALTHY BOUNDARIES

Having permeable boundaries that are 'holey' or fragmented or weakened by not knowing how to say 'no' can leave you vulnerable to incursion by other people's energies and especially to them 'pulling your strings' to get you to do what they want or 'pressing your buttons' to wind you up or hooking into your energy field for a top-up of their own energy, none of which is conducive to inner peace.

If your boundaries are healthy and strong, nothing and no one can disturb your inner serenity, no matter how much they may try. This does not mean having inflexible boundaries. It's not conducive to your well-being to be cowering within a defensive wall with your heart firmly closed and a big 'Keep Out' sign on the front – unless it's an emergency, but even then you can be courageously sheltered within your crystallized boundary with an open heart. If you have healthy boundaries, your heart is open and you can empathize with others and invite them into your heart knowing you'll experience only good in the process.

So what causes our boundaries to become weak? Physical damage or scarring can be reflected in the aura and can affect your ability to hold your energy together and prevent psychic leakage. I once worked with a woman who was aware of a sense of weakness in her left side. She felt she lost energy in that part of her body and was constantly depleted, especially by contact with needy people. Some years previously she'd been involved in a car accident and had a visible scar. Seen clairvoyantly, the energy below her left arm was grey and ragged, leaving her open to psychic vampirism as the energy flow around her body, and her aura, was blocked. The area over the site was weak and vulnerable. Energy could 'leak' out. Hematite, which is magnetic, was stroked over the site to return the aura to its normal magnetic vibration and heal the break. This was followed up with the Australian Bush Flower Essence Slender Rice Flower, which heals physical scarring. Her energy quickly became stronger.

Checking out your aura quickly reveals whether you have weaknesses or 'holes'. For these next two exercises a helpful friend would be useful, but you can do them yourself with a little improvisation and focused intention.

WHERE'S MY AURA?

Your aura, the subtle biomagnetic energy sheath that extends out from your body, is your natural boundary. If it goes too far out (and it can extend for quite a distance), people interpenetrate it all the time and can pull on your energy or infuse you with negativity and gloom. If it's brought in too tightly, it doesn't have enough room to do its work of filtering energies before they reach you physically. A comfortable distance is about arm's length all around your body, but if you feel 'invaded' you can pull it in closer and protect it with the Bubble of Light (*see pages 20–21*) or the Amber Melt (*page 206*). As your aura is one of the tools your intuition uses to suss out people and places, having it extend to a sensible distance helps you to feel safe and gives you the best chance of spotting anything untoward before it reaches you. Fortunately you can easily take charge of this process.

Treasure Chest

SELENITE

Crystallized divine light, ethereal white Selenite occupies the space between light and matter. It's an excellent stone for repairing and re-energizing the aura. It holds a deep inner peace and meditating with it takes you into pure light and creates a protective grid around an area, as it does not allow outside influences to penetrate. A large piece within the house ensures a peaceful atmosphere prevails.

FLUORITE

A strongly protective stone, especially against electro- and geo-pollution, Fluorite stabilizes energy. It shuts off mental manipulation and cleanses the aura.

Try This: Checking your Aura

Ask your friend to walk towards you with hands outstretched. Try to feel when your aura is touched by the hands. Consciously think about extending your aura out further and get your friend to check it out, pull it in closer and check again. You'll quickly gain control of how far out this auric field extends. If you're using your own hands to monitor it, you will be able to push or pull your aura with your hand.

Thank your friend for the assistance and take over the process of checking yourself. You can either use your hands or a crystal for this part of the process.

You can also repair 'holes' or weak places in your aura with a crystal and detach 'hooks' from people who are embedded within your auric field. Again, this should be done with focused intention.

Try This: Repairing your Aura

- Stand comfortably so you can reach all around yourself (sit if you find this easier).
- Take a cleansed Charoite, Flint, Selenite or Clear Quartz crystal and, starting at arm's length above your head, gently brush all over your aura with your crystal. (If you cannot physically reach around your back, the power of your mind will do this for you.)
- If the crystal hesitates or drops inwards, or you feel a cold patch or sense a hook or a cord-like obstruction, take your time and ask the crystal to dissolve the hook and repair the hole with light. Spiralling the crystal out, flicking it and spiralling it back in helps this process.
- When you've checked out the outer levels of your aura, work a little more closely in towards your body, and then more closely still, until you're sure your aura is healthy and whole.

Sometimes the alignment between the physical body and the aura 'slips' a little, resulting in a sense of not being comfortable within your body. It is variously described as feeling not quite yourself or having a sense of disequilibrium or disharmony or even of standing outside yourself. Indications vary and can include irritability (physical and emotional), 'buzzing' or discomfort in the body or ears, and 'flu- or ME-like symptoms. If this is the case, you can often feel the energetic dis-ease in your aura – a bit like getting an electric shock or sensing 'waves' or 'bumps'. Combing over your aura with an appropriate crystal can realign it with the physical body and restore equilibrium, as can holding Amber over your head (*see page 206*) or solar plexus and asking to be realigned.

Crystal Tips for the Aura

- *Quartz and Selenite cleanse, repair, align and re-energize the aura, but other crystals can be helpful such as Amber, Bloodstone, Flint, Green Jasper, Herkimer Diamond, Rainbow Mayanite and Smoky Quartz.*
- To protect the aura: *Amber, Amethyst, Apache Tear, Diamond, Healer's Gold, Labradorite, Lemurian Jade, Quartz, Shattuckite with Ajoite (wear continuously).*
- To align your aura with the physical body: *Hold Amber over your head or solar plexus.*
- To align your aura spiritually: *Hold Labradorite or Green Ridge Quartz over your head.*
- To guard against energy leakage: *Black Tourmaline or Labradorite (wear constantly).*
- To repair 'holes': *Amethyst, Aqua Aura, Green Tourmaline, Quartz, Selenite.*

- To remove negativity: *Amber, Apache Tear (hold the crystal over your solar plexus), Black Jade.*
- *Green Ridge Quartz cleanses and realigns the whole chakric and auric systems.*

Crystal Tips for the Aura
Crystal Balance Violet Flame transmutes negativity into positivity and protects the aura. Dream Catcher is excellent for protecting children's auras.

You can also use a version of the vision board (**Tool 19, page 49**) to strengthen your aura. Draw or place a picture of yourself in the centre and around it place a rainbow of coloured light, pictures of crystals and anything else that makes you feel totally centred and protected within your aura.

Additional Tools
Guardian Angel (**Tool 17, page 44**), Psychic Shields (**Tool 18, page 47**).

CAN YOU SAY 'NO'?
Being able to say 'no' when being put upon, emotionally manipulated or asked to do something inappropriate for your highest good is an excellent means of protection.

- Ask yourself how easy you find it to say 'no' and write the answers in your journal.
- Picture yourself in various scenarios and with different people such as family, friends, employers, employees and so on, and see how saying 'no' feels with them.

- Make a list of who makes you feel vulnerable, where it's difficult to say 'no' and the emotions or feelings behind that inability to stand your ground. You'll be able to work on transforming these later in the book, but if you cannot wait turn to page 65 or 147.

Treasure Chest

BRAZILIANITE

Brazilianite is one of the newer stones coming, as the name suggests, from Brazil. Its brilliant green colour supports your boundaries and assists you in saying 'no' – and meaning it. It also helps to manifest abilities that would normally seem to be superhuman. It facilitates taking responsibility for yourself and moving forward confidently, having accepted long-denied vulnerability and negative emotions. It also promotes forgiveness. It teaches you how to find your core strength and heals a black hole in your emotional centre.

Try This: Saying 'No'

- Now practise saying 'no'. This is where a helpful friend comes in handy again. Ask your friend to walk towards you trying to manipulate, sweet-talk, wheedle, bully, badger and hector you into saying 'yes'. (If you don't have anyone to take this part, use a mirror and your imagination.)

- Stand with your hands firmly in front of you, palms out and elbows bent, at chest height or shoulder height, whichever is more comfortable. Push your hands forward, saying 'no' firmly but quietly until they are a comfortable distance from your body.
- Keep saying 'no' firmly for as long as necessary.

Additional Tools

Journalling (*Tool 6, page 19*), Psychic Shields (*Tool 18, page 47*).

YOUR PSYCHIC IMMUNE SYSTEM

Your psychic immune system works in tandem with and is linked to your physical immune system, the endocrine system and the different energetic frequencies of the subtle biomagnetic sheath – your aura – that encloses your physical body.

THE CHAKRA SYSTEM

The chakras are energy linkage centres that connect your physical body with the subtle bodies contained within your aura. They distribute the life-force (often known as *prana* or *Qi/chi*) through the physical and subtle bodies and are the basis for holistic healing. If a chakra becomes blocked, the subtle energy flow becomes imbalanced and dis-ease or disharmony eventually results.

Specific issues, toxic emotions, mental states and positive or negative qualities can be supported or ameliorated by placing an appropriate crystal on the relevant chakra or chakras. While a rainbow of colours is often applied, this is a relatively modern invention and there are many crystals that have traditionally been used to support the chakras that don't follow this colour scheme.

Traditionally seven major chakras are recognized, but as consciousness is raised, so more chakras become available, many of which have been known since ancient times.

The Chakras and their Functions

Earth (Root)
• *Position:* Below the feet.

- *Function:* Grounding and protecting, cleansing and stabilizing.
- When this chakra is working positively, you're grounded and operate well in everyday reality.
- When it is blocked or working negatively, you're ungrounded, have no sense of personal power, cannot operate in everyday reality and easily pick up negativity from the environment.

Base

- *Position:* The base of the spine/perineum.
- *Function:* Energizing and motivating, sharpening the survival instincts, basic security, your sense of your own power.
- When this chakra is working positively, you're active, independent and lead spontaneously.
- When it is blocked or working negatively, you're impatient, fear annihilation, have a death wish, feel over-sexed or impotent and are vengeful, hyperactive, highly impulsive, angry, violent and manipulative.

Sacral

- *Position:* Below the navel.
- *Function:* Creation, fertility, procreation and manifestation.
- When this chakra is working positively, you have courage, assertion, confidence and joy, enjoy sensual pleasure and accept your sexual identity.
- When it is blocked or working negatively, it can lead to infertility. You have low self-esteem and may be cruel or sluggish, feel inferior or be pompous. This chakra can be the site of emotional hooks or thought forms from other people.

Solar Plexus

- *Position:* Above the navel.
- *Function:* Nurturing, emotional connection and assimilation.
- When this chakra is working positively, you have good energy utilization and are empathetic, organized and logical with active intelligence.
- When it is blocked or working negatively, you have poor energy utilization, feel lazy, are overly emotional or cold and cynical, carry emotional baggage and suffer from energy leaching, easily taking on other people's feelings and problems.

Heart

- *Position:* Over the physical heart.
- *Function:* Love, healing, empathy, overcoming emotional distress.
- When this chakra is working positively, you're loving, generous, compassionate, nurturing, flexible, self-confident and accepting.
- When it is blocked or working negatively, you're disconnected from your feelings, unable to show love, jealous, possessive, insecure, miserly and resistant to change and mired in emotional pain.

Higher Heart

- *Position:* Over the thymus.
- *Function:* Links all the chakras with unconditional love and compassion. Connects to universal love.
- When this chakra is working well, you're compassionate, empathetic, nurturing, forgiving and spiritually connected.
- When it is blocked or working negatively, you're

spiritually disconnected, grieving, unable to express feelings and emotionally needy.

Throat

- **Position:** Over the throat.
- **Function:** Communicating and expressing feelings.
- When this chakra is operating positively, you're able to speak your own truth with clarity and are receptive, idealistic and loyal.
- When it is blocked or working negatively, you're unable to verbalize your thoughts or feelings, feel stuck and can be dogmatic and disloyal.

Brow/Third Eye

- **Position:** Above and between the eyebrows.
- **Function:** Attuning to psychic abilities and the subtle energy world, providing mental intuition and connection.
- When this chakra is open and working well, you're intuitive, perceptive, visionary and in the moment.
- When it's blocked or working negatively, you're spaced out, fearful, attached to the past, superstitious and bombarded with other people's thoughts.

Soma

- **Position:** At the hairline above the third eye.
- **Function:** A point of connection between the incarnating spirit, the physical body and the divine.
- When this chakra is open and working well, you feel spiritually connected and comfortable in incarnation, aware of your purpose and your lifeplan.
- When it is blocked, you feel alienated and ungrounded and are unable to raise your consciousness to a higher level.

Crown

- *Position:* The top of the head.
- *Function:* Opening intuition and spiritual communication.
- When this chakra is working positively, you're mystical, creative, humanitarian and willingly give service to others.
- When it is blocked or working negatively, you're overly imaginative, delusional, arrogant and use power to control others.

Higher Crown

There are a number of higher crown chakras, including the soul star and stellar gateway, that link to higher aspects of your soul and your higher self or other dimensions.
- *Position:* Above the crown.
- *Function:* Opening spiritual communication and reaching enlightenment.
- When these chakras are working positively, you're spiritually connected, attuned to higher things, enlightened and have true humility.
- When these chakras are blocked or working negatively, you are spaced out and open to invasion, illusions and delusions and are unable to distinguish between spiritual reality and cosmic cons. (*See page 223 for opening the higher chakras.*)

Cleansing and Recharging your Chakras

When chakras are out of balance or blocked, they tend to pulsate at a slower or faster rate than usual and may well 'wobble' or spin in a reverse direction. However, as different people's chakras naturally spin in different directions, do not assume that because a chakra is not spinning in the direction someone says it should it is out of balance. A great deal of harm can be done by a well-meaning but dogmatic person 'regulating' your chakras to conform to what they believe is the right direction of spin. It may not be right for you and may damage your natural protection.

Fortunately a crystal will quickly pick up any imbalance and cleanse and re-energize a chakra, rectifying any blockage as it does so.

For a Fast Chakra Cleanse...

- Work with a long-pointed crystal – Clear, Laser or Lemurian Quartz is ideal – and start at the base chakra, with the point out.
- Rotate your crystal over the chakra in a circular fashion, pulling the energy out to at least an arm's length.
- Cleanse the crystal and rotate the energy back in the opposite direction, with the point pointing in.

Note: There are no strict rules about the direction in which you should rotate the crystal. Just do whatever feels right to you at the time.

Crystals are also useful for a full chakra cleanse and recharge. You can lay them on yourself (*see below*) or ask a friend to help you. Remember to cleanse them first.

For a Full Chakra Cleanse, Balance and Recharge...

- Lie down comfortably where you will not be disturbed.
- Place Smoky Quartz or another cleansing, earthy stone between and slightly below your feet. Picture light and energy radiating out from the crystal into the earth chakra for two or three minutes and be aware the chakra is being cleansed and its spin regulated and rebalanced.

- Place Red Jasper or another energizing crystal on your base chakra. Picture light and energy radiating out from the crystal into the chakra as before.
- Place Orange Carnelian or another energizing crystal on your sacral chakra, just below the navel. See the light and feel the cleansing and rebalancing process taking place.
- Place Yellow Jasper or another emotional cleansing stone on your solar plexus.
- Place Green Aventurine or another heart cleanser crystal on your heart.
- Place Blue Lace Agate or another blue stone on your throat.
- Place Sodalite or one of the third eye openers on your brow.
- Place Amethyst or bright Clear Quartz or Selenite on your crown.
- Now draw your attention slowly from the soles of your feet up the midline of your body, feeling how each chakra has become balanced and harmonized.
- Remain still and relaxed, breathing deeply, inhaling and counting to ten before you exhale.
- As you breathe in and hold, feel the energy of the crystals re-energizing the chakras and then radiating out through your whole being.
- When you feel ready, gather your crystals up, starting from the crown. As you reach the earth chakra, be aware of a grounding cord anchoring you to the Earth and to your physical body.

(See page 223 for opening the higher chakras when you are ready.)

THE IMMUNE SYSTEMS AND DIS-EASE

Psychic self-protection isn't only concerned with putting up a shield or drawing off negative energy, it's also about ensuring your psychic and physical immune systems are functioning at their optimum level. As your immune system is the first line of defence against invading organisms or energies, finding the right balance between an under- and overactive immune system – physical or psychic – is crucial.

There are several factors that can knock the immune system off balance. If you receive any kind of shock, whether it's at the physical, emotional, mental or spiritual level, your chakras quickly go out of balance, your immune system crumbles and your body reacts by going into 'fight or flight' mode and flooding your system with adrenaline. Physical, emotional or mental shock occurs when you are present at violence, disaster, trauma and tragedy. Psychic shock can come about by watching horrific scenes on television, especially if you imagine yourself a part of them, or hearing about something horrendous that sets off your imagination and worst fears. It can arise from walking into a negative energy field, either one set deliberately for you or left behind by someone – 'psychic mugging'. It can also occur, as can spiritual shock, when you are out of your body or during healing or meditation that is not working at the highest level for your highest good. It can arise through deliberate psychic attack, or ill-wishing, which comes out of someone turning their anger or negative thoughts or emotions towards you. If you are attacked, whether by physical viruses or by someone's thoughts, dis-ease results and equilibrium needs restoring.

Stress and tension are also powerful initiators of dis-ease. Inadequate rest and nutrition, stressful living, constantly having to meet deadlines and indeed anything that puts a continual stress on your physical or psychic immune systems ultimately manifests as dis-ease of one kind or another.

How you think, or feel, is how you'll ultimately become in your physical body. Toxic emotions such as guilt, shame or suppressed anger are insidious precursors to dis-ease, as are chronic feelings of low self-esteem and victim mentality. Continually blaming yourself, especially for things you can in no way control, is equally lethal. Guilt and shame are nasty shocks to the subtle levels of your being. All these affect both the psychic and physical immune system.

If you've been continually drained at an emotional level, by a person or a situation, whether by their behaviour or demands or by a more subtle form of energy leaching, you'll have lowered resistance to dis-ease. Paying attention to the spleen point under your left arm and removing any energy hooks or drains is vital (*see page 117*).

Chronic anxiety and constant fear also weaken the physical and the psychic immune systems. Chronic anxiety is often accompanied by loss of appetite or by gut conditions that preclude the proper absorption of nutrients, and irregular sleeping patterns add to the strain, which may be exacerbated by smoking or drinking.

If depression is a consequence of toxic emotions, medication may suppress the underlying feelings, again causing dis-ease.

Environmental pollution can also create energetic dis-ease that affects the physical and psychic immune systems. Wireless networks, communication masts and so on have a marked effect on the immune systems and sleeping patterns of susceptible individuals.

Many of these factors either deplete the immune systems or force them into overdrive. Fortunately, all of these effects can be reversed and your immune systems can be strengthened in a balanced way that will enable you to resist dis-ease at whatever level it occurs.

Treasure Chest

VARISCITE

This stone is perfect if you want to understand the causes that lie behind dis-ease or illness of any kind and to find a pathway of healing. One of the great stones of encouragement, it assists invalids and their carers to have hope and to trust in the ultimate goodness of the universe.

Crystals for your Immune System

The major crystal healing point for your physical immune system is the thymus gland, situated over your higher heart chakra, in the centre of your chest about a hand's breadth below your collarbone, and this is a linkage point for your psychic immune system too.

Bloodstone, Que Sera and Quantum Quattro are excellent stones for balancing both immune systems. If a system is overactive, they sedate it. If it's underactive, they stimulate it. At the first sign of an invading dis-ease, tape one of these stones over your thymus and leave it in place for several hours. Similarly, if you suffer a shock or feel particularly stressed, place one on the thymus to alleviate the dis-ease.

Treasure Chest

QUE SERA

An all-round healer and re-energizer, this powerful, synergistic combination has extremely high and yet deeply earthy vibrations. Que Sera is a powerful carrier of Qi and is an excellent shield against Wi-Fi emanations and other electromagnetic pollutants and geopathogens. It recharges and balances the meridians and organs of the subtle and physical bodies. If you have a tendency to dwell on problems this crystal helps you find constructive solutions and to be confident about your actions. This stone helps you co-create your own future.

Try This

To stimulate the immune systems, place an immune stimulator (*see below*) on your thymus and an Apophyllite or Clear Quartz in the centre of your forehead, and lie with your hands on each side resting in your groin crease for ten minutes, holding a Smoky Quartz.

Alternatively, tap over your thymus with a Bloodstone or other immune system stimulator for about 20 taps.

Crystal Tips for Immune Stimulators
Amethyst, Bloodstone, Clear Quartz, Green Aventurine, Quantum Quattro, Que Sera, Rose Quartz, Shungite, Smithsonite, Sodalite.

Additional Tools
Affirmations (*Tool 13, page 36*), Crystal Layouts (*Tool 2, page 14*), Visioning (*Tool 14, page 37*), Happiness (*Tool 25, page 59*), Crystal EFT (*Tool 27, page 65*).

FOILING THE ENERGY PIRATES

Another important point for the psychic immune system is the spleen point, located under your left arm. Psychic vampirism – people pulling on your energy to feed their own – occurs here. You often become aware of it because of a nagging pain along the ribs under your left armpit or a sensation of tugging on this spot. These energy pirates may be people you know or have known, or those who are just passing through. Therapists and others who work with needy people are particularly vulnerable to energy pirates and it may well be necessary to learn how to protect yourself (taping a Green Aventurine over the spot is useful, as is visualizing a green pyramid from the armpit to your waist, *see page 24*).

Energy Drain Signals
• a sudden loss of energy
• a nagging pain or tugging below left or right armpit
• the inability to sleep
• continual overwhelming tiredness

Previous partners can be a continuing source of energy vampirism, even some years after the relationship has ended. Two friends of mine were experiencing energy loss and vague niggling plains under the left arm but didn't, at the time, attribute it to anything in particular. They went to see a healer who immediately said that their ex-partners were still hooked in. He removed the hooks and they visualized green pyramids over their spleens, but they also found they needed Green Aventurines to complete the protection. They knew that it had worked when both their ex-partners, on the same day, managed to sever the power cords to electrical equipment with which they were working without being harmed!

I would also use Z14 to clear any etheric ties and cleanse the subtle levels of being and check that any higher chakra connections have also been disconnected – these are particularly vulnerable if you and your ex were involved in spiritual work together.

Energy drains are often connected to such 'hooks' into your spleen that need to be removed and you can use Clear or Laser Quartz, Rainbow Mayanite, Nuummite, Flint or Novaculite (exercise caution as these latter stones are usually in the form of sharp shards) to cut the cords from your body and a piece of Rose Quartz or Green Aventurine to heal the site afterwards.

If you become aware that being around a certain person, speaking to them on the phone or by e-mail or simply thinking about them drains your energy, you're probably tied together energetically by one of these energy drains. This can arise with partners, families, friends, clients or work colleagues, but the exercise below will soon release you.

Dealing with an Energy Drain

Try This: Cutting an Energy Drain Quickly

- If you become aware of energy drain signals, ask yourself, 'Where or whom does this come from?' (There are times when someone whose energy is attached to the person you're with is actually creating the drain and you may experience it when you are seemingly alone, *see page 122*). Allow the name to come to mind spontaneously, don't strive for it.

- Disconnect it by rotating one of the energy drain-cutting crystals over your spleen point (just below your left armpit), or taping a Green Aventurine there, and sealing the place with light.
- Protect the left side of your body with a green pyramid (*see Tool 8, page 23*).
- Even if you don't know who the drain comes from, disconnect it and protect yourself. If you don't have a crystal handy, use an imaginary, virtual one.

Here is another exercise:

Try This: Cutting a Known Energy Drain

- If you know who is draining your energy, picture them in your mind's eye. Visualize a cord linking the two of you together from your spleen point under your left arm to wherever in the other person the cord leads – usually the heart, solar plexus, reproductive organs or throat (check whether there are other cords and deal with those later).
- Take a big pair of gold scissors and cut the cord away from yourself, then continue chopping it into little pieces until you reach the other person. Visualize a plaster of healing light over the place where the cord was attached to your body and one on the other person. If the cord goes deep into your body, image a laser scalpel or a piece of Laser Quartz cutting it out and place a plaster of healing light over it.
- Check there are no more cords, particularly around the spleen and reproductive areas or the

liver point under your right armpit. If there are, deal with them in the same way.

- Picture the cut-up cords being put onto a big bonfire and transmuted.
- When all cords have been dealt with, place yourself inside a bubble of light (*Tool 7, page 20*) or a golden pyramid (*Tool 8, page 23*) to safeguard your energy field.
- Allow unconditional love and forgiveness to go to the person who was draining you. Look on them with compassion.
- Bring your attention back into the room and ground yourself again.

If you're a touchy-feely (kinaesthetic) person:

- Take a piece of cord and a large pair of scissors.
- Place a photograph of the other person at one end of the cord and hold the other end yourself.
- Firmly chop the cord into pieces.
- If you wish, chop the photograph into pieces also. This won't harm the other person. The pieces can be burned or shredded and composted.
- Or use Crystal Balance Detachment Spray.

You can extend this energy release by making a vision board to remind you of and maintain your energetic freedom.

Try This: Using a Visioning Board

- To remind yourself that you are now free from this energy drain, paste a photograph of yourself into the centre of a vision board.

- Around it draw your bubble of light or big green pyramid.
- Outside the bubble or pyramid, at the edge of the board, draw or paste feet walking away out of your space, broken chains and anything else that symbolizes your freedom from the energy drain.

Afterwards, whenever you meet the person causing the energy drain, check your bubble of light (*see Tool 7, page 20*) or the green pyramid (*see Tool 8, page 23*) is in place so that the cord does not reattach. It would be sensible to tape a Green Aventurine, Fluorite, Gaspeite or Jade over your spleen point and wear either a Black Tourmaline or Yellow Labradorite crystal over your thymus when you're with them to provide additional support until you're sure you've regained control over your psychic immune system.

It is also possible that, having cut off the energy loss from the spleen point, you may begin to experience a stabbing pain under the right armpit. This will be because the 'vampire' has realized that the energy piracy has been foiled and become angry. If this occurs, protect the liver point with Gaspeite or Tugtupite.

Crystal Tips for Cutting an Energy Drain

- *Apple Aura Quartz, Clear Quartz, Flint, Green Aventurine, Green Fluorite, Green Jade, Laser or Lemurian Quartz or Novaculite on the spleen point.*
- *Gaspeite or Tugtupite on the liver point for anger following disconnection.*
- *Use Crystal Balance Detachment Spray.*

Moving on Stuck Spirits

Sometimes the energy drain comes from a 'stuck spirit', someone who has died but not moved on, whether because of unfinished business, leaving too quickly, a desire to retain control over the living or simply because they have lost their way.[7] Sometimes they don't even know they are dead – after all, they feel very alive! They may wonder why everyone around them appears to ignore them and may do all they can to gain attention, which can make them something of a nuisance. There are also times when these apparently lost souls are actually thought forms that have taken on a life of their own (*see page 125*).

Releasing such souls requires a professional spirit release practitioner (*see Resources and Further Reading*), but there are times when you have to use emergency measures. If you're moving on a stuck spirit, ask that they be taken into the light to the guides and helpers who are waiting to assist further.

Treasure Chest

GREEN AVENTURINE

Green Aventurine is an excellent stone for preventing energy loss to energy pirates or due to electromagnetic stress. A stone of prosperity that opens and calms the heart, it's a useful gridding stone against environmental pollution. It assists you to see and assess alternatives and possibilities and promotes emotional recovery.

Treasure Chest

RAINBOW MAYANITE

A self-cleansing stone, Rainbow Mayanite is a Golden Healer taken to new heights. With exceedingly high vibrations, this is not a stone for the inexperienced. Rainbow Mayanite de-energizes old patterns from any source, taking out debris and karmic encrustations from the past, and pulls out toxic dross absorbed from other people or the environment from your aura. It can also release stuck souls or thought forms. It then creates a non-penetrable interface around the outside of the aura. It continues to repattern the energy field to its optimum functioning and highest frequency. This stone takes you into the depths of yourself to discover your own inner rainbow treasures. It works in different ways according to its natural shape. In chunky points it is a gentle support for energetic change and is suitable for those who are new to high-vibration crystal work. As a blade Rainbow Mayanite needs to be used with delicacy in the hands of a skilled healer. Pieces that combine both shapes, blades and chunky points, work on all levels simultaneously and are perfect for gem essences for multi-dimensional and intercellular healing.

Try This Only If You Have to:
Moving on a 'Ghost' or Lost Soul

- Place a few drops of Astral Clear or Special 8 on a clear Quartz crystal and leave in place for a few hours with the intention that it will dissolve the imprint. Leave the room after doing so.
- Alternatively, place a large Ametrine, Candle Quartz or Aventurine crystal in the room and ask for the spirit to be moved on.

This often moves a lost or stuck spirit on, but some lost souls can be deeply troubled and are often caught up in an outdated intention or worldview, and these souls really do need professional help. Their unfinished business may include a powerful desire for a substance. If so, telling them it's still available in the etheric world is usually sufficient to move them on, but it may be more serious. Often asking them to write a letter to someone of whom they need to ask forgiveness or to explain why a promise could not be kept and so on is sufficient to help them on their way. As they are sometimes unaware they have passed to another realm of existence, you may have to enlighten them, but only do it if your boundaries are strong and your confidence is high.

Try This Only If You Have to:
Moving on a Stuck Spirit

- Sit quietly, put yourself in a bubble of light (*see Tool 7 page 20*) and focus your attention on calling in higher helpers and guides to assist you.

- Holding one of the crystals listed below, ask that the spirit be taken to the light by their guardian angel. This works well if the spirit has simply lost the way home. Petaltone Astral Clear or Z14 essences or a dedicated Aventurine or Candle Quartz can be effective clearers, as can burning a candle in a church and asking that the soul be forgiven, if appropriate, and taken home to the light.

- Sometimes simply knowing it is in the post-death state is all a spirit needs to move on of its own accord, but you may need to do more. Check out whether this is actually a lost soul who needs to be returned to the spirit world or whether it is a thought form that needs to be dissolved – a Laser crystal, Rainbow Mayanite or Petaltone Clear Tone essence assists with this.

- If you can communicate with the spirit, ask if there is anything you can do to assist and what they need. Surprisingly perhaps, the requests are often simple and easy to arrange, and frequently relate to unfinished business or forgiveness. Once you've agreed to do or offer whatever is required, the spirit moves on.

- It may be the spirit is still stuck in the viewpoint or purpose it had while alive. If so, check whether this purpose is still appropriate. Release may be achieved by helping the spirit to take a different view, particularly turning around to look at how things were in the past and how they have changed. (This is particularly useful when a relative is still protecting a 'child' even though that child is now an adult.) Asking the spirit to write a letter and send it over the ether also works well.

• If the spirit is deeply entrenched, or is still of the opinion that its advice and assistance are crucial for the well-being of someone still on Earth, calling in an expert is your best course of action, but do choose someone who moves spirits on to an appropriate place rather than just banishing them elsewhere to bother someone else. Your local Spiritualist church, shamanic practitioner or metaphysical centre will be able to help. In the meantime, keep your own energy high to ensure you're well protected.

Crystal Tips for Lost Souls

Aegirine, Candle Quartz, Flint, Quartz, Novaculite, Nuummite, Rainbow Mayanite, Rose Quartz, Smoky Amethyst, Smoky or Amethyst Brandenberg, Spirit Quartz, Super 7.

Essences for Lost Souls

Bush Boab made into a spray with Angelsword, Fringed Violet and Lichen; Petaltone Astral Clear, Z14 or Special 8.

DETOXIFICATION

If your body is toxic, it cannot maintain physical health. Similarly, if your etheric body is toxic it cannot maintain psychic health – and holding on to negative emotions or noxious thought patterns creates subtle toxicity.

Stimulating your liver with detoxification crystals releases toxins and encourages your lymphatic system to remove them, bringing about a physical and psychical cleansing. It's particularly helpful if you follow this up with a salt bath, gently scrubbing your skin with a loofah or bristle brush or a piece of Halite and working from the feet towards the heart and from the top of the head towards the heart. Adding a Smoky Quartz or Yellow Jasper at your solar plexus stimulates an emotional detox at the same time, but drink plenty of water and have some tissues handy in case tears flow, which is an excellent form of release.

This detoxification layout* gently releases and neutralizes toxicity on all levels:

The Detoxification Layout

• Place Smoky Quartz between your feet.
• Place Yellow Jasper over your solar plexus.
• Place Bloodstone and Amethyst over your thymus.
• Place Red Jasper over your liver (base of ribs on right side).
• Place Sodalite at the base of your throat.
• Leave in place for 15 to 20 minutes, breathing gently and letting go on all levels as you do so.
• Cleanse the crystals thoroughly after use.

* The Detoxification Layout can also be found in *Crystal Healing* and *Crystal Experience* (both published by Godsfield Press), together with further detox techniques.

Salt and Halite

Salt is another traditional cleanser and protector that has been prized for centuries – it was frequently sprinkled around doorways to keep unwanted guests at bay. Many people use it to cleanse crystals, but you must ensure these are not layered or friable, as it can cause them to disintegrate. It also needs to be cleaned off any crystal carefully, as it may scratch.

Halite is the crystallized form of rock salt.

Try This: Instant Detox

Place a couple of handfuls of salt in the bath or hang salt under a showerhead in a small bag, or use a piece of Halite to purify your energies or to pull toxins or negativity from your body.

It's possible to make detoxifying a more ceremonial occasion, one that provides a powerful detox and a time for deep relaxation, like this detox bath. Be sure to drink plenty of cool pure spring water during and after it.

Try This: The Detox Bath

- Light pink candles and place them around your bath.
- To a teaspoon of sweet almond or olive oil add three drops each of Scots pine and juniper essential oils and pour over two large handfuls of Dead Sea Salts (or sea salt).
- Add the oil-infused salts to your bathwater and soak in it for as long as possible. As you do so, chant rhythmically to yourself, 'Letting go, letting go, deeply letting go,' to remind yourself of the purpose of your bath.

- This mixture pulls out toxins from your body, which can become very hot – you may need to place a cool cloth on your face or to suck ice.
- It can be helpful to shower yourself off afterwards and spray yourself with an aura spray such as Soul Shield by the Living Tree Orchid Essences.
- Repeat for several days.

If you feel light-headed during the bath, take your attention down to your feet, hold a piece of Hematite and visualize the toxins leaving your body and white healing light flooding in to assist the detoxification process, filling up the spaces where the toxins have been. You can also add a piece of Bloodstone to the bathwater to boost your immune system at the same time.

Here are some other ideas for baths:

- *The Immune Booster Bath:* Add two handfuls of Dead Sea Salt or sea salt to the bathwater in which you've placed a piece of Bloodstone, Quantum Quattro or Smithsonite at each corner and a piece of Yellow Jasper under your back, level with your solar plexus.
- *The Invigorating Bath:* Add three drops each of rosemary and geranium essential oils to the almond oil and sea salt and place a Carnelian, Poppy or Red Jasper in the water at your base chakra.
- *The Relaxation Bath:* Add four drops of lavender essential oil to the almond oil and salt and place Amethyst or Rose Quartz in the water over your heart.

Detoxing your physical body will almost immediately begin to reveal the emotional or mental toxins you've been holding in your body, or indeed any places where you are still carrying dis-ease in your body, as these will be sore or achy. In which case, Crystal EFT is the next stage of the detox process.

EMOTIONAL DETOXING

Tap Away your Negative States

As we have seen, if you're holding on to negative emotions or are trapped in behaviour patterns that don't serve you, you'll constantly manifest difficult situations that create exactly the conditions you fear. And if you're stuck in an obsessive or toxic thought process, you'll attract people whose emotions and behaviour mirror the toxicity. The fastest and most effective way to transform these noxious situations I've found is Crystal EFT. The following information is taken from my book *Good Vibrations*, but I feel it bears repeating here because it's such a gift to be able to enhance your self-protection so rapidly.[8]

As we've seen, Crystal EFT uses specific 'tapping points' on the energetic meridians of your body to identify and clear negative emotions, toxic thoughts and destructive behaviour patterns. Tapping with a crystal heightens the transformation. As you tap, you say a statement out loud to reprogramme the energy.

Crystal EFT can also be used for physical conditions and feeling safe when travelling. It's excellent for any fears or phobias you may have, as it sets you free (you may need several sessions of tapping to uncover the deepest cause of your phobia). It can also put you in touch with ingrained thoughts, angers and toxic emotions that have lurked in the depths of your subconscious mind without you noticing and have attracted physical and social situations that mirror that toxicity.

Although the instructions are to tap each point seven times, it really doesn't matter if you do six or eight, as you'll get into your own rhythm as you tap. It can be quite confusing when you first start trying to count, tap and say your statement all at the same time, but don't worry. That's part of why it works! It takes you out of your rational, everyday mind and allows the emotions and feelings to surface in your body and realign themselves through the energetic meridians and chakras. Counting and saying the statement gives your brain something to focus on – our brains need to be entertained to stop them going too much into 'head stuff' and especially to stop them censoring what we need to feel and say. So, in a way, the more mentally confused you are, the better, as that helps the feelings to flow, the toxic thoughts and emotions to surface and the old patterns to reveal themselves.

In addition to absorbing negative energy, using a crystal such as a Brandenberg or Lemurian Seed Quartz restores your subtle energy grid to the perfect energetic state it had before a pattern, thought or emotion became ingrained, which is why Crystal EFT adds in an extra tapping point, the soma chakra that links to that perfect energy grid. Whichever crystal you use, cleanse and dedicate it before use and cleanse it afterwards.

Points are tapped with the flat or rounded end rather than the point of the crystal to avoid the possibility of injury. Some points need to be tapped using all the fingers, in which case, hold the crystal in the palm of your hand with your thumb. The tapping points are illustrated opposite. If two points are available, tap whichever side is easiest. You don't have to tap both sides or follow the order rigidly, although you can do. The more you go with the flow, the better. Tap with whichever hand feels more comfortable; it really doesn't matter which you use and you can switch in the middle if that feels better.

The Tapping Points

- **'Karate chop':** The outer edge of the hand (tap with all the fingers of the other hand).
- **The crown chakra:** The top of the head (tap with one finger or crystal).
- **The soma chakra:** The centre of the forehead at the hairline (tap with one finger or crystal).
- **The third eye:** At the centre of the forehead slightly above the eyebrows (tap with one finger or crystal).
- The inner corner of the eyebrow (tap with one finger or crystal).
- The outer corner of the eyebrow (tap with one finger or crystal).
- Below the centre of the eye (tap with one finger or crystal).
- Below the nose (tap with one finger or crystal).
- The centre of the chin (tap with one finger or crystal).
- **The 'sore spot'** on the collarbone either side of the breastbone (tap with thumb and fingers either side).
- **The spleen chakra:** Under the left armpit (tap with all fingers).

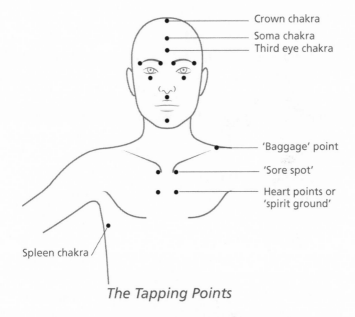

Crown chakra
Soma chakra
Third eye chakra

'Baggage' point

'Sore spot'

Heart points or 'spirit ground'

Spleen chakra

The Tapping Points

Each point is tapped seven times, or thereabouts, and there may be times when your hand wants to reverse the direction, moving back up from the spleen point towards the head, for instance, or simply dancing around in a spiral. If you allow them to, your crystal and your intuition will guide you. I cannot emphasize enough that you should do what feels right to you.

Other places on your body may also call out to you to be tapped. Simply go with the flow and tap without needing to know why that specific point has called to you. If a point particularly needs tapping, it is sore when you touch it. Tapping releases and transforms the negativity stored in that point and you can replace it with beneficial energy and positivity.

Useful points for emotional or spiritual pain and mental or emotional baggage:

- *Heart points or 'spirit ground':* Either side of your breastbone about a hand's breadth beneath your collarbone, just above the breasts in women and slightly higher than the nipples in men. (Tap with all the fingers.)
- *The 'baggage' point:* About halfway along the top of your shoulder (tap with all your fingers and you'll soon find it). Tap both shoulders.

The Set-up Statement

Working with Crystal EFT begins with a 'set-up statement' that emerges from a rant that is as deeply negative and pessimistic as possible. Don't be afraid to exaggerate and never censor what comes into your head – this is one time when being deeply negative actually is of benefit.

Say out loud everything you think and feel about the issue that has provoked you, while tapping the side of your hand with your crystal, which absorbs the negativity. Tap for as long as you want. Don't try to keep count of the taps or to censor what you say, just tap and allow the words to come. The more negative you are at this stage, the more you 'go with the flow' by allowing a stream of consciousness rant to emerge from your mouth without thinking about it, the more dramatic the transformation – and the more hidden, unconscious beliefs, toxic thoughts and emotions surface and are absorbed by the crystal.

Remember to wrap any other person concerned in a cloak of pink light and remind yourself that you're dealing with your own inner reactions, not the person themselves, and send unconditional love and forgiveness to that person afterwards.

The set-up statement identifies the core issue or feelings you're working on. From the stream-of-consciousness rant something key will emerge. It can be generic, 'Feeling unsafe', for example, or specific, 'Fearing being attacked.' It can also be enormous anger or hurt or jealousy or sadness or loneliness or a deep sense of lack that has no name, in which case simply keep saying: 'I am so angry [or whatever], I am boiling, pulsating with rage, so very very angry [or whatever], I want to…' and allow whatever wants to come roaring out of your mouth to do so. You may be surprised at what you're really angry or sad about – small triggers can release huge wells of ancient anger and pain. If this happens, go with it, keep talking and keep tapping. Ask yourself: 'When did I first feel this anger/ pain/jealousy/sadness/etc.?' and allow the answer to rise up spontaneously rather than seeking it with your head.

An example is given below to help you create your own set-up statement, but it's important to use your own feelings and thoughts rather than following this exactly.

Carry out at least three rounds of tapping. With each round, the statement becomes more positive, allowing for change and transformation, but if you need to go back to being deeply negative and pessimistic because something hasn't quite released or surfaced, do so. If that occurs, remember to ask yourself: 'When did I first feel/ experience/think this?' and tap on what comes up.

Your personal set-up statement is always followed by:

'Nevertheless, I deeply and profoundly love, accept and forgive myself unconditionally and completely,'

although you can change the order of the words if you wish. This is the key to emotional healing. Using a crystal also supports you in forgiving and loving yourself deeply and unconditionally; crystals are love solidified and a crystal joyfully transfers that love to you. If you find you're ranting at someone else, you can add that you deeply and unconditionally love, accept and forgive that person as well.

For some people, particularly when negativity has had a deep but unconscious hold, becoming positive can feel very scary indeed, so the more you can love, accept and forgive yourself during the process, the more you will support yourself in allowing change.

Using a crystal during the tapping encourages you to empty those toxic spaces and fill them up with new light and positivity. You'll know it has worked when you stop attracting into your life situations and people who mirror or provoke those old fears, negative emotions and toxic thoughts. But, until you do, keep tapping on issues and feelings that emerge, remembering they are helping you to get to the bottom of things and transform the depths of your being. Having said that, Crystal EFT can work amazingly quickly, especially when you've the strong intention of letting go and transforming and are able to do the work and indeed let go.

Tapping
The next round of tapping follows on from the tapping and stream of consciousness rant that established your set-up statement:

• Saying your initial set-up statement out loud and
   holding the crystal against the palm of your hand,
   tap the fingers of one hand firmly against the 'karate

chop' point on the side of the other hand seven times, or whatever feels right to you. (You may prefer to rub the 'sore spot' on the collarbone either side of the breastbone. If the 'sore spots' are really sore, they work well for you.) Repeat your set-up statement several times while tapping, allowing whatever words come into your mind to be spoken and being as deeply negative as possible. Remember to say: 'Nevertheless, I deeply and profoundly love, accept and forgive myself unconditionally and completely' at the end.

• Choose a word or short phrase that is shorthand for your issue. It may change as you move through the points, but just allow whatever needs to be said to come out of your mouth. Reassure yourself that there is no one right way to do this; you can do and say whatever works for you.

• Saying out loud your shorthand phrase and starting with the top of your head, tap each point (one side only or both as you feel is appropriate) as shown on the diagram seven times or so with the crystal, allowing your hand to move freely between the points if this feels appropriate.

• Check out how you are feeling. If the feeling is still strong, tap all the points for two more rounds, allowing changes in the wording to emerge spontaneously as you tap. Cleanse your crystal if this feels appropriate.

• Rephrase your initial set-up statement to allow for change and become more positive.

• 'Karate chop' the side of your hand seven times or so whilst repeating this new statement out loud, again allowing any changes or unconscious phrases to be spoken but adding the final phrase.

• Using your rephrased shorthand or anything that comes to mind as you move between points, do another round of tapping on each point on one side of your body, starting at the top of the head and finishing under the arm, or following the instinct of your hand guided by the crystal.

• Repeat two more rounds of tapping if necessary, allowing changes in wording to emerge spontaneously as you tap.

• Make the third and final statement as positive as possible, finding the opposite to your original feeling. If you've been working on timidity, the opposite could incorporate, 'Brave, fearless, forceful,' for instance. If you've been working on feeling unsafe, the positive could be: 'Totally safe, fully protected.'

• Do another round of tapping, saying your final shorthand and again finish with: 'And I deeply and profoundly love, accept and forgive myself unconditionally and completely.'

• Sit quietly for a few moments reviewing how you feel and enjoying the change you've brought about. If you're using a Brandenberg, place it over your heart as you do this.

• If appropriate, do two more rounds of tapping, allowing spontaneous changes in the words to emerge. Cleanse your crystal.

Repeat the tapping night and morning, or at any time when you feel a need, until the transformation is complete, but check out whether you're getting into another pattern and trying to keep control, which is all too easy to do. Some people become addicted to tapping in the same way that they are addicted to their toxic emotions. You may find that the set-up statement changes, revealing an underlying issue of which you were unaware. If that happens, do a fresh set of three rounds of tapping to transform that issue and remember to unconditionally love, accept and forgive yourself as you do so.

Here's a crystal EFT example to help you:

• *Identified issue:* Not feeling safe at night.

• *Set-up statement on 'karate chop' point:* 'I've never felt safe at night, have always worried something would happen, have always been fearful about everything, terrified of my own shadow, frightened of the dark, sure something terrible was going to happen to me, that I'd be mugged, that my house would be broken into, that my car would be stolen... I've always been terrified by a knock on the door after dark, haven't liked going out after dark, haven't liked staying in much either, have always lain in bed with the light on, worried there was something under the bed, haven't liked travelling, especially after dark, haven't even liked walking from my car to the house, have been frightened to death of car parks, and even though I've never been able to overcome this and I don't think I ever will, and even though I hate feeling unsafe in the dark, and even though every time it's dark I am afraid, nevertheless I deeply and profoundly love, accept and forgive myself unconditionally and completely.'

• *Shorthand for tapping points:* 'Feeling unsafe.' Tap all the points.

• *Rephrased set-up statement on 'karate chop' point:* 'Even though I haven't felt safe in the dark in the past, it's possible to feel safe now. Even though I have always been afraid to go out when it was dark, I choose not to be afraid now and choose to take what I always saw as a risk in the past because I now feel safe. And in choosing to feel safe, I deeply and profoundly love, accept and forgive myself unconditionally and completely.'

• *Rephrased shorthand for tapping points:* 'Choosing to feel safe.' Tap all points (include the spirit ground and 'sore spots' if these feel appropriate).

• *Final statement for 'karate chop' point:* 'I feel safe and protected and happy to go out at any time. I have chosen to let go of fear and I no longer allow fear and feeling unsafe to ruin my life. I am brave, totally safe and protected and live my life fearlessly and with full enjoyment and trust. I embrace the dark. I am trusting and safe and I deeply and profoundly love, accept and forgive myself unconditionally and completely.'

• *Shorthand tapping points:* 'Totally safe, fully protected.' Tap all points.

Crystal EFT often brings about a profound change from the first time you use it, but you may need to repeat the tapping several times, allowing deeper issues to surface. You can do this within the same session, or in different sessions that are carried out whenever you notice yourself having a negative thought or toxic emotion. Don't feel you've 'got it wrong' or it hasn't worked if you do find yourself back in the old pattern, this is merely a sign that you need to uncover a deeper issue. Go back into the stream of consciousness flow, exaggerating the negativity and allowing whatever lies in the deepest recesses of your mind to surface, and remembering to follow with the key phrase: '*Nevertheless, I deeply and profoundly love, accept and forgive myself unconditionally and completely.*'

Re-visioning with Crystal EFT

You can also use Crystal EFT to help you re-vision a past situation or experience that is causing you grief today. Do three rounds of tapping with focused intention, the first going through the situation as it happened in all its awfulness (and remember that this word can also be written 'awe-fullness', so pat yourself on the back for having survived it). The second round identifies all the changes you want to make to what happened and the different outcome you want to achieve. The third round then puts it all into the present tense so that it changes what happened back there in the past. Remember to love, accept and forgive yourself all the way through.

RELIEVING STRESS
••••••••••••••••••••••••••

Stress can occur at the physical, emotional, mental or even spiritual level. It takes an enormous toll on your subtle bodies and affects both the chakras and the psychic and physical immune systems. Regular meditation or relaxation helps to keep your stress levels down and your inner being calm (*see Tool 4, Relaxation Crystals, page 17, and meditation, page 217*).

When you're under stress, your adrenal glands, which sit on top of your kidneys, go into 'fight or flight' mode, overproducing adrenaline. This is nature's way of giving you additional strength to overcome occasional difficulties, but nowadays many people suffer continual stress, which results in burnout because, if this adrenaline isn't removed from your body, you end up feeling wired and find it impossible to sleep or relax.

Try This: Reduce your Adrenaline Load

Green Aventurine, Eye of the Storm, Gaspeite and Rose Quartz prevent the overproduction of adrenaline and reduce the feeling of being wired. Green Aventurine aids mental stress and Rose Quartz emotional stress, but the two complement each other and work in tandem while Eye of the Storm is complete in itself. Place Rose Quartz over your left kidney and Green Aventurine over your right, slightly above your waist a hand's breath either side of your spine. Or place Eye of the Storm or Gaspeite here. Leave in place for 15 minutes to reduce an adrenaline high or burnout.

If you've been keeping your journal, you'll probably already have identified several causes of stress that you hadn't recognized previously. Even things that you enjoy doing, such as sport, can bring about stress if you're constantly playing to win rather than enjoying the game.

'Freehand' spontaneous journalling can also identify further stresses in your life:

Try This

- Head a page 'Stressors' and write several lines below which say: 'It stresses me out when…' You may immediately have something to write, in which case fill in the blank, or write a dozen or so beginnings and go back and fill them in. You'll find the process gets quicker as you give up censoring how you should be feeling or what you should be enjoying and begin to be truthful with yourself.
- Once you've got your list, go through them and see how many you can transform by using positive affirmations. If, for instance, you identify that you always play to win at sport and put extra pressure on yourself to win even when you might feel like taking it easy and simply enjoying the game, ask yourself who told you that you had to win every time. Is it your own competitive nature or were you programmed with this directive early in life? You can use the affirmation 'I play to enjoy the exercise and the skill I bring to the game' and whatever else you identify as a positive benefit, team spirit and so on.

Once you take the stress out of situations and begin to enjoy yourself, you'll find that paradoxically your confidence increases and you feel better. This in turn benefits your psychic self-protection, as your immune system and especially your adrenal glands won't have to work so hard to protect you.

Crystals for Stress Relief

Crystals are also useful for rapid stress relief. Palm stones are your gift from the crystal kingdom. These gently rounded stones fit snugly into your palm and bring instant peace. Keep one in your pocket and play with it when you feel stressed or nervous. Fluorite is particularly effective as it not only relieves mental stress and helps you to think more clearly, but it also protects against computer and other electromagnetic sources of stress. Leave yours on the computer when you need both hands for your work and you'll see an immediate difference in how you cope.

Try This

Lying or sitting quietly for 15 minutes with an appropriate crystal helps you to release stress.

Crystal Tips to Reduce Stress

- General stress: *Amethyst, Bloodstone, Clear Quartz, Eye of the Storm, Labradorite, Nunderite, Richterite, Rose Quartz, Smoky Quartz, Shungite, Yellow Jasper.*
- Mental stress: *Dioptase, Green Ridge Quartz, Kunzite, Lepidolite, Quantum Quattro.*

Additional Tools

Happiness (*Tool 25, page 59*), Relaxation Crystals (*Tool 4, page 17*) and meditation (*see page 217*).

THE ENERGY RECHARGE

If you're tired or lacking in energy, you'll also be more vulnerable to other people's moods or to the emanations of place and this can deplete your immune system. Fortunately a quick exercise soon re-establishes your core body energy levels.

Treasure Chest

CARNELIAN

An excellent stone for grounding you in present reality, Carnelian is one of the oldest known healing stones. It energizes and restores vitality to the immune system. Promoting positive life choices and immense motivation, it also assists in trusting yourself and your perceptions.
This is a useful stone for overcoming negative emotional or mental conditioning.

Try This: The Energy Boost

- Lie with your feet slightly apart and your knees bent a little so that your feet are flat on the floor or bed. Let your arms hang loosely by your sides and place your fingers in a v-shape below your belly button.
- With each in-breath, draw energy up from the grounding cord that goes from your feet deep down into Mother Earth, focusing the energy and drawing the breath deep into your lungs and focusing it into your hands.

- Allow the energy to collect just below your navel and with each out-breath spread it to all levels of your being.

Treasure Chest

POPPY JASPER

A powerhouse that is gently stimulating or fiery as required, Poppy Jasper is a strongly physical stone that bring vitality and passion, grounding energy into the body and stimulating libido or soothing an overactive libido. It instils fresh motivation and imparts the courage to get to grips with problems assertively. Sustaining and supporting during times of stress, calming the emotions.

Crystal Tip

Pop a Carnelian, Eye of the Storm or Poppy Jasper in your pocket and hold it when you need extra energy. Note that Crystal Recharge also recharges your energy and Grounding Spray anchors you, while Crystal Balance's Light spray feeds your energy.

TRANSMUTING TOXIC EMOTIONS

As we've seen, toxic emotions affect both your sense of security and your psychic immune system, but there are many ways of transmuting them.

NEGATIVE TO POSITIVE

When you're writing in your journal, whenever you identify a negative or toxic emotion or become aware of a mental pattern that is wearing you down, get into the habit of finding the opposite, positive quality and writing it in large letters next to the negative so that it becomes a positive affirmation. This can help you to re-vision your life. For example:

- Anger = Forgiveness and compassion
- Anxiety = Serenity
- Fear = Trust and intimacy
- Poor me = Empowered me
- Sadness = Joy
- Victim = Victor
- Worry = Tranquillity and acceptance.

Try This: Identify the Positive

There are times, however, when emotions, thoughts and feelings are all mixed together and can't really be separated. To help you to identify the positive quality and find the gift in any experience, you could productively spend five minutes trying to pair the

NEGATIVE
abandonment
abuse
aggression
anger
anxiety
apathy
boredom
codependency
confusion
criticism
dependency
despair
despondency
destructive tendencies
emotional baggage
envy
failure
fear
grief
guilt
hatred
impatience
inadequacy
inferiority
intolerance
irritability
jealousy
obsessions
narrow-mindedness
lack of inspiration
lack of motivation
lack of purpose
limitations
manipulations
over-attachment
overreacting
overspending
overstimulation
overworking
self-doubt

POSITIVE
attunement
compassion
empathy
forgiveness
freedom
happiness
generosity
honesty
hope
independence
joy
nurturing
patience
acceptance
potential
empowerment
peace
responsibility
centredness
competence
tolerance
innocence
open-mindedness
calmness
confidence
determination
inspiration
connection
groundedness
expression
security
authority
wisdom
perseverance
motivation
clear-sightedness
faith
unconditional love
introspection
abundance

positive and negative qualities in the list opposite and see how you get on. To make you think a little more about the process, the list doesn't give the corresponding positive quality for every negative one. So if I haven't listed the opposite quality, identify it for yourself. It reminds you that for every negative there is a positive. Enjoy!

TOXIC EMOTIONS AND THE CHAKRAS

Toxic emotions can be lodged in your chakras or the subtle bodies that comprise your aura. Fortunately, placing appropriate stones on your chakras helps to transmute these negative emotions into positive ones. As the negative emotion can be deeply ingrained, the crystal should be taped in place or the placement repeated at least once daily for a week or more until the emotion is fully released.

As the crystal is placed, visualize it pulling the negative emotion from your physical body and the subtle bodies, and filling the space with its unique healing vibration.

Also, always remember to draw bright white light or gentle Rose Quartz energy in to seal where the emotion has been released to avoid leaving a vacuum that might be filled by another negative energy, and be aware that when you release energies in this way you can feel rather empty, as though there's a hole in the part of your body where the emotion was held. Re-energizing with a crystal helps to fill this hole, as does the inner smile (*Tool 25, page 60*).

Negative Emotion	Chakra	Crystal	Positive Emotion
Powerlessness	Earth	Smoky Quartz	Empowerment
Insecurity	Base	Red Jasper	Security
Low self-esteem	Sacral	Orange Carnelian	Self-confidence
Inferiority	Solar Plexus	Yellow Jasper	Connection
Jealousy	Heart	Green Aventurine	Compassion
Neediness	Higher Heart	Rose Quartz	Unconditional love
Disloyalty	Throat	Blue Lace Agate	Loyalty
Self-delusion	Brow	Sodalite	Emotional clarity
Alienation	Soma	Brandenberg	Acceptance
Arrogance	Crown	Clear Quartz	Joy

CRYSTALS FOR EMOTIONAL BALANCE

Wearing or surrounding yourself with crystals helps to keep your emotions in balance as well as gently releasing the emotional blockages or suppressed feelings which cause your moods to fluctuate. Crystals draw out difficult emotions. They can be taken as a gem essence or, as we have seen, placed over the appropriate chakra.

Crystal Tips for Emotional Balance

- *Amethyst gently dissolves emotional blocks, balances out emotional highs and lows, and encourages emotional centring.*
- *Eye of the Storm quietly absorbs stress and toxic emotional blockages, transmuting them into safe space within your heart.*
- *Rose Quartz calms and reassures. Strengthening empathy and sensitivity, it assists you to understand how other people feel and how that affects*

you. *Excellent for releasing unexpressed emotions and healing heartache, it transmutes emotional conditioning that no longer serves you. This stone comforts grief and helps self-forgiveness and self-worth.*

- *Smoky Quartz stabilizes your emotions during emotional trauma or stress and dissolves negative emotions, facilitating emotional detoxification. Assisting in tolerating difficult times with equanimity, it is excellent for relieving fear and promoting emotional calmness.*

Try This

Place a Rose Quartz over your heart, a Smoky Quartz over your solar plexus and an Amethyst over the higher heart chakra and leave in place for 20 minutes to restore emotional equilibrium, or, for specific issues, use one of the crystals below.

Crystal Tips for Releasing Anger
Place over base chakra:

- *Amethyst dispels anger and deep-seated rage, transmuting them into a loving energy, and can dispel the grief which often underlies rage.*
- *Bloodstone reduces irritability, aggressiveness and impatience and all forms of anger.*
- *Blue Lace Agate gently dissolves anger, replacing it with profound peace.*

- Carnelian calms anger and is helpful for moving beyond abuse (which can also cause feelings of impotence and powerlessness).
- Green Aventurine calms anger and irritation and promotes an overall feeling of well-being.

Crystal Tip for Dissolving Guilt

A Blue Lace Agate placed on the base, solar plexus and brow chakras releases your suppressed feelings and frees you from the judgement so often inherent in parent–child relationships and so often a source of guilt.

Crystal Tips for Healing Past Hurts

Place over the base, sacral, solar plexus, heart and throat chakras:

- Amethyst: dispels fear and anxiety and alleviates sadness and grief. It helps you to adjust to any loss you may have suffered, wiping away pain and grief.
- Blue Lace Agate also releases you from situations where you felt rejected and, if you are a man, helps you to accept the sensitivity for which you may have been ridiculed in the past.
- Mangano Calcite is excellent for overcoming the pain of abused childhood or lost love. It brings unconditional love into the heart to replace guilt, self-doubt and lack of love.

Crystal Tips for Healing the Pain of Being in Incarnation

Place over the base, sacral, heart and soma chakras or tap the spirit ground points:

- A Brandenberg, Dalmatian Stone, Eye of the Storm, Green Ridge Quartz, Pearl Spa Dolomite, Quantum Quattro or Snakeskin Agate crystal helps you to adjust to physically being in incarnation.
- In addition, a Brandenberg adjusts the subtle energy grid contained within your aura to the most perfect balance possible, releasing any toxic imprints, injuries or memories.

OVERCOMING FEAR

Fear is perhaps the most insidious enemy of all and is constantly being talked up by the media and advertising and the people around you. The world appears hazardous, full of threats and traps such as poverty, and you come to feel something – or even everything – is out to get you. Lose the fear and all possibilities are open to you. One of the greatest favours you can do yourself right now is to give up engaging with doom-mongering or people-belittling media and concentrate on programmes or news with a positive slant. (Remember that you can crystal tap to remove any fears. It is particularly effective with phobias.)

Treasure Chest

CHAROITE

A stone of transformation and vibrational shifts, Charoite is the crystal associated with the astrological 'planet' Chiron that helps to integrate and heal wounds from the past. This stone is excellent for releasing deep fears and overcomes resistance to change, putting things into perspective. A stress reducer, it assists you in overcoming compulsions and releasing yourself from other people's thought control.

Try This: Find and Overcome your Fears

- Cleanse a Charoite, Eye of the Storm or Rosophia crystal and sit quietly holding it in your hands. Tell yourself that you're willing to look honestly and openly at your fears, acknowledge them, feel them fully and let them go. Ask the crystal to help you to identify and overcome them.
- Look deep into the stone. See how the colours blend and fold together. Choose one of the lines and let it lead you inwards to the root of your deepest fear. Follow the twists and turns of the line as it takes you deep into yourself to reveal the fear hidden there. Let the name of that fear come into your mind and say it out loud.
- Sit quietly with the feeling of that fear for a while. Just be with it, don't try to banish it, allow it to be.

Treasure Chest

ROSOPHIA

Rosophia facilitates self-healing for body and soul and grounds spiritual energy as it has a very profound earth connection. Strengthening your rational and analytic thought processes, it helps you discard what is irrelevant and concentrate on the important detail. This stone is particularly helpful for strengthening and raising the energies of the lower chakras so that you feel more comfortable in incarnation and adapt to the energetic changes, maintaining constant equilibrium. A pure stone of the heart, Rosophia opens all the heart chakras. You literally live from your heart in love in the present moment.

- As you sit with the fear, feel how the crystal supports you, giving you reassurance and allowing you to fully feel the fear. Keep feeling the fear until it gently dissolves away and is no longer there.
- Ask the crystal to show you what the positive side of that fear is, what gift it holds for you now you've let it go. Say the gift out loud, let it take the place of the fear in your inner self, and anchor it in the crystal so you are reminded of the gift whenever you hold the stone.
- You can either choose to explore another line to find another fear or to come out of the contemplation and return to it another time.

- When you've finished your contemplation, bring your attention fully back into the room, ground yourself by feeling your feet on the floor and holding the stone for a few moments to centre yourself and strengthen your boundaries and your root.

Remember to write up your experience in your journal and to re-vision any negative situation in the past.

If you have fears of which you're aware or would like to try another stone, choose an appropriate crystal from the list below.

Crystal Tips for Overcoming Fear
Amazonite, Amethyst, Azurite (for when old belief systems create fear), Blue Lace Agate (for when you fear being judged by other people), Calcite, Candle Quartz, Carnelian (for when you fear death), Charoite, Chiastolite (for when you fear going mad), Citrine (for when you feel unsupported by the universe), Diamond, Dumortierite, Eye of the Storm, Fire Agate, Jet, Labradorite, Leopardskin Jasper, Mangano Calcite, Mariposite, Moss Agate, Orange Calcite, Orchid Calcite, Rosophia, Tugtupite.

Additional Tools
Affirmations (***Tool 13, page 36***), Positive Thought (***Tool 16 page 42***), Guardian Angels (***Tool 17, page 44***) and Crystal EFT (***Tool 27, page 65***).

OFFERING AND RECEIVING FORGIVENESS

One of the most powerful ways to heal emotional dis-ease, toxic emotions or mental obsession is through offering and receiving forgiveness, or simply radiating forgiveness out to the world, no matter who is at fault. Indeed, if you can find it in yourself to forgive those you feel have wronged you, you'll benefit enormously and find inner serenity.

The gentle energies of Rose Quartz help you to forgive both yourself and other people and replace the anger or hurt with unconditional love and acceptance, leading to spiritual peace.

Try This: The Forgiveness Ceremony

- Hold your Rose Quartz between your heart and your higher heart chakra.
- Picture the person whom you feel you need to forgive or from whom you seek forgiveness (you can use a photograph if you have one).
- Be aware of the unconditionally loving energy of the Rose Quartz radiating out into your higher heart chakra and from there into your heart. Be aware that this energy is also pouring into the other person's heart.
- Say out loud: 'I forgive you and I accept your forgiveness. I offer you unconditional love and acceptance. Go in peace.'
- When you feel ready, put down the crystal, but keep it close to remind you of the forgiveness.

This ceremony is particularly potent if you are able to share it with the person with whom you wish to give and receive forgiveness. Stand together and place a Rose Quartz over each other's heart and proceed as above.

DRAWING OUT TOXIC EMOTIONS

Holding toxic emotions anywhere in your body is like having a faulty seal around a hosepipe. Either the water can shoot out in all directions or gunge can leak in and contaminate the water inside. This means you can 'leak' emotions and contaminate other people or be depleted yourself, or be vulnerable to toxic environments. So, pulling out that emotion gives you a leak- and invasion-proof aura and makes you psychically invulnerable. Here are some ways to do it.

Visioning

I've been using this particular visioning process for drawing out toxic emotions for over 45 years now and I've added crystals to assist with transmuting the emotions. It has a powerful effect and, for a short time, it can feel as though there are huge holes within you through which some very cold winds are blowing. Indeed, there are times when you feel as though you're being torn to shreds and little of you remains (rather like the shamanic death initiation in which a shaman is torn to pieces. This is a gentler process but nonetheless profound.) If you can stay with that feeling while you complete the process of drawing out the toxic emotions and releasing your emotional baggage, it brings about a powerful transformation at the deepest level of your being.

This is a process to be carried out when you have the confidence that you're ready for this radical re-vision of your inner being. If you have any doubts, wait until you've worked through some other exercises in the book and come back to this when you've more confidence in your abilities.

If you begin this work but find you cannot complete it in one session, always go to the final part of the exercise, steps 6–8, to heal and seal the places where you've let go with light. Each time, it becomes a little easier.

A Lemurian Quartz wand is ideal for this process, as is Green Ridge Quartz, but as they are expensive you may prefer to use a Clear Quartz or a Tibetan Black Spot wand. Remember to cleanse and programme your crystal before starting and whenever it begins to feel 'heavy' during the process.

Try This: Drawing Out Toxic Emotions

- *Step 1:* Settle yourself comfortably, having ensured you won't be disturbed, and hold your crystal wand in whichever hand feels comfortable. Ask your guardian angel (*Tool 17, page 44*) to be with you and to hold a safe space in which you can work. Breathe gently and withdraw your attention from the outside world and into yourself.
- *Step 2:* Picture a meadow or another favourite spot such as a beach. You need a place where you can have a big bonfire blazing. Now allow yourself to be transported into that place, really feel and smell the air and the bonfire and the earth beneath your feet. Take time to get yourself fully acquainted with the place.

- **Step 3:** Put the whole space and your guardian angel into a big bubble of light to protect you.
- **Step 4:** Take your attention round your body and wherever you feel you have a stuck emotion or a blockage, use the crystal wand to dissolve it and to release the memory that underlies it. If you find it comes out in the form of dirty bandages or cotton wool (a common occurrence), put the bandages onto the fire to purify and transform the energy. Make sure you go all over your body, all around the back as well and deep within yourself. Allow the cold holes to simply remain as they are for the moment, but if they feel really unbearable, place a plaster of light over them.
- **Step 5:** When you've cleared your body, take a look around your favourite spot and see if you've stashed any emotional baggage under bushes, behind rocks or in any of the other possible hiding places. Collect it up into a big pile.
- **Step 6:** Take the baggage to the fire and throw it on. As you do so, be aware of letting go with love and forgiveness but vow to yourself never to take it back. Watch as the baggage is transformed by the purifying fire. Notice how much lighter you feel when you've let go all your baggage.
- **Step 7:** Draw as close to the fire as possible and allow the transformed and purified energy to come back to you to heal and seal all those cold holes within yourself. Feel it re-energizing you and transmuting your inner being into one of unconditional light, love, compassion and forgiveness.

- **Step 8:** When the process is complete, thank your angel for being with you. Dismantle the bubble of light around your favourite place and bring your attention back into the room. Put your own bubble of light in place, stand up and ground yourself thoroughly with the grounding cord. Cleanse your crystal thoroughly.

REVERSING MENTAL OVERLOAD

Negative or obsessive thinking is one of the most destructive things you can do to yourself – or to other people because, if you obsess on their behalf or about them, you'll attract to them what you most fear for them. Rigid thinking, deeply inculcated beliefs, negative expectations and self-doubt are weapons you turn against yourself or others.

How you think generally and what you expect on a day-to-day basis can have a surprising effect on the inanimate objects around you, as this story shows:

'I had to go to the hospital to hear the test results for my young son. If the news was bad, it would require an operation and long hospitalization, so it was a tense and emotional journey.

Within a few minutes of leaving the house the car started misfiring and juddering and I drove for the next 40 minutes with the car stalling at every junction. In the end, I abandoned it and walked the last few hundred yards, shaking with anticipation as I went.

After receiving the good news from the doctor that my son wouldn't need an operation, I decided to give the car another try before calling my husband for assistance, as I was a long way from home. It started first time and I drove home with not a single stall. I realized then how much my fear had been affecting the car.'

Similarly, what you read, what you fantasize about and where you put your mental energy can create situations which sometimes feel like an external mental influence but may not be.

Some years ago a young man came on one of my workshops. He was psychically open and traumatized following repeated sexual abuse in a psychiatric hospital when he was a teenager. He had, he believed, picked up a 'spirit' there who was particularly unpleasant with a strong sexual focus. This alleged 'spirit', he claimed, had taken over his thoughts and feelings and he had become obsessed with sex and sexual fantasies. Having dealt with people with similar feelings, I began to wonder whether this was in fact a spirit. Although it communicated, its vocabulary and content were limited. The same information repeated itself, all of it linked to sexual fantasy of abuse. I asked for details of the life the spirit had lived on Earth, but there was no answer. Then I asked the young man to try using a psychic light technique to 'zap' the spirit. It instantly dissolved. It had been a thought form – something created by words and thoughts rather than a living being. My feeling was it had been created from the young man's experience of abuse and his constant dwelling on it. As he was so psychically open, he had absorbed his abuser's fantasies, carried the energy around with him and strengthened it by paying attention to it as a spirit rather than recognizing it was his own memories. Whilst he clearly needed further counselling work to overcome the effects of the abuse, the fact that he had finally owned the memories rather than projecting them onto a 'spirit' meant that he would be able to deal with them.

Treasure Chest

SUNSTONE

If pessimism or another negative mental attitude is your problem, a glinting, glitzy Sunstone is your answer. Encouraging optimism and enthusiasm, it switches to a positive take on events. Even the most incorrigible pessimist responds to it. It's particularly beneficial when worn in the sun, as this doubles its effect. This stone is excellent if you suffer from the lethargy of seasonal affective disorder and long for the summer sunshine to lift your dark moods.

DISPELLING MENTAL NEGATIVITY

Apathy, hopelessness and helplessness are insidious mental attitudes that have a deeper effect than might at first appear. They underlie poverty, despair and victim mentality. The world looks bleak, the person 'suffers' and it is all someone else's fault. But by taking responsibility for your feelings and mental attitude, 'failure' or 'lack' can be turned into a positive gift for the future. Take the decision now to become a thriver, not a victim or merely a survivor, and note it in your journal.

But you can also become mentally obsessed with something, a fear for the future or of illness, a belief system you have bought into without really thinking it through, or some of the more bizarre manifestations of this world of ours. Any such obsessions need to be released if you are to fully protect yourself psychically.

To find out what mental patterns or ingrained thoughts you carry, adapt the journalling technique on page 19 and turn the patterns into new affirmations.

Treasure Chest

SONORA SUNRISE (CUPRITE WITH CHRYSOCOLLA)

This stone is excellent for reframing destructive emotional or mental patterns from any timeframe and for feeling safe in all situations. It eases the mind with regard to situations over which you have no control and strengthens trust that all is well. Overcoming difficulties with authoritarian figures, it releases rigid 'oughts and shoulds' and mind control. Sonora Sunrise offers great vitality and strength.

Cut the Worry

Next to fear, worry is the greatest underminer of all your plans. Constant worry actually creates the situations you fear. As much of it is generated from listening to so-called experts, stop believing what they tell you and find out for yourself, as knowledge equals power. Above all, cut the worry!

Worry beads have been used for thousands of years to help calm and focus the mind. Letting the beads slip through your fingers while in a relaxed state facilitates new insight into the most difficult of situations and helps to rectify unjust situations. Red Jasper makes excellent worry beads. This stone helps you to see what really matters and what is an unnecessary concern. It also strengthens your boundaries and helps you to say 'no'.

Try This: Worry Beads

Gently slip a string of worry beads through your fingers while quietly contemplating your worries and allow them to dissolve with each click of the beads. This will soon bring you to a calm place.

Additional Worry-Bead Crystals

Amazonite, Azurite, Eye of the Storm, Pink Crackle Quartz, Rainbow Obsidian, Ocean Jasper, Rose Quartz, Smoky Quartz, Snakeskin Agate.

Additional Tools

Make a list of worries in your journal and turn them into positive affirmations (*see Tool 6, page 19 and Tool 13, page 36*).

Try This Ceremony: The Worry Pot

- Sit quietly and on a small rainbow pad, with focused intention, write each of your worries on a separate piece of paper. Write everything, no matter how big or small, that is concerning you. Some may seem trivial and silly, others absolutely overwhelming, but put them all down on paper.
- Use a fireproof pot or make a fire and, taking one worry at a time, set fire to the paper and drop it in the pot or on the fire. As you do so, say out loud: 'I release this worry to the universe so it can be taken care of for me.'

- Watch the paper burn away and add the next one until all the worries have gone up in smoke.
- Feel how the weight of those worries has lifted from your shoulders, stand up tall, smile and say out loud: 'I am free, untroubled, and I trust in the universe.'
- Turn your attention elsewhere.
- If you find yourself worrying again, write down the worry and burn it.

Additional Tools

Pink light (*see page 199*), programming a crystal (*see page 12*).

What Exactly is the Problem?

It can be really difficult at times to ascertain exactly what is causing a problem, particularly as a strong belief on someone else's part may influence what is 'seen' as the reason for certain behaviour. This case history is an old one that I have used before, but it is one of the most graphic and illuminating I have come across and it bears repeating.

Many years ago now, when I was first training as a healer and psychic, a boy was brought to the local Spiritualist church healing group for an exorcism. His parents, and the church's minister, were convinced he was possessed by an evil spirit. There had been a great deal of poltergeist activity in the house, and the boy was depressed and suicidal.

The minister put his hands on the boy's shoulders and began the exorcism, repeatedly telling the spirit to be gone. I became aware of this spirit. He was a lost soul, a boy of about the same age as the other boy. He told me he'd been attracted to the boy because they shared many feelings. Some of the poltergeist activity was his, as he was trying to attract attention so the boy would know he had company. But it was not him who was causing the boy to feel suicidal, nor were the more frenetic poltergeist manifestations anything to do with him.

I asked that his guides and guardian beings come and take him to the light. He told me he'd been able to see the light and had heard people calling him, but did not know how to get there, so I told him to look around for the person who had come to fetch him. When he found this person, he went willingly into the light. In the light he would receive healing and be able to look back at his life on Earth and his choices for the future.

The minister, who had continued to exhort the 'evil spirit' to leave, pronounced that the 'exorcism' was complete, the spirit had gone. He did not think the boy would have any further trouble.

But he did.

I was training to be a teacher at the time and on a school visit I met the boy again. He was still feeling suicidal. In fact, as he said: 'I actually feel even more bereft now, as I felt that spirit cared about me.' He went on to tell me that his parents, although sharing the same house, lived separate lives, one upstairs and one down, and never spoke to each other. They used him as an intermediary. His father kept a loaded shotgun beside his bed and more than once had threatened to kill himself 'because of her'. Despairing, the boy had once picked the shotgun up and threatened to kill himself instead. The energy in the house was, in his words, 'poisonous'. His parents were extremely angry with each other and that anger festered in the house, rising to peaks which coincided with the worst of the poltergeist activity – activity which frightened the boy.

I suggested to him he should visualize a bright shiny new dustbin into which he could jump at the first sign of trouble. We also worked on strengthening his aura and giving him protection on a day-to-day level. He quickly learned the pyramid meditation to create a safe space in his bedroom, where he spent most of his time.

I knew the local educational psychologist was a sensitive and open-minded man with a particular interest in this kind of phenomenon and its causes, both psychic and psychological, so I suggested he might be able to help. His psychological counselling did help the boy to find his own inner equilibrium.

Later, the boy was able to attend a sixth-form college as a boarder. As soon as he did so his parents split up – a great relief for everyone concerned. They had constantly told him – separately – that they were only staying together for his sake and he'd carried an enormous amount of guilt as a result, guilt that was literally depressing him. Once he was at college, he had no further trouble with poltergeists or depression. Moving out of that poisonous atmosphere was all he needed to feel psychically and therefore psychologically and physically healthy.

So, don't be too quick to think you have sussed out the cause of your psychic vulnerability, as there may well be hidden or underlying conditions that need time to gently float to the surface. When they do, you can use the tools you now have to transform them into positive activity.

CRYSTALS FOR HEALING MENTAL PROBLEMS

Crystals can be an enormous support if you suffer from mental problems such as an obsession with fearful thoughts, and they can stabilize your mood or assist you to overcome addictions or other compulsive patterns, particularly as they help you to deal with the underlying cause of your problem.

You can wear your stone constantly to support your mind or carry crystals with you, grid them around your space or make gem essences for various mental conditions (*see Tool 5, page 18*), as these are particularly effective for gently dissolving the subtle underlying causes behind them.

Try This: Get Motivated

If you feel uninspired or unmotivated, try wearing a sunny Citrine, Poppy Japser, Quantum Quattro, Sunstone or Topaz. These crystals shed golden light on your purpose and inspire limitless possibilities. Your motivation gets a kick start whenever these powerful crystals are nearby!

Crystal Tips for Specific Conditions

• Addictions: *Amethyst has a sobering effect and is helpful in overcoming addictions or overindulgence of any kind. It was traditionally worn to ward off drunkenness and to provide protection. (Use cider vinegar to preserve the essence if you have an alcohol addiction or allergy.) Use Botswana or Fire Agate if the addiction is to nicotine.*

- Anger: *Angry thoughts can be as destructive and debilitating as the emotion itself. Soothing Agate gently dissolves the kind of bitter anger that eats away inside you and leads to compulsive thinking. If you choose the Blue Lace variety, you'll find it calms and lifts your thoughts and has the added benefit of opening your throat chakra so that you can communicate your feelings clearly. Keep a piece with you at all times and hold it whenever anger threatens to overwhelm you.*
- Anxiety: *Amethyst, Covellite, Crackle Quartz, Epidote, Halite, Mangano Calcite, Kunzite, Rutilated Quartz/Angel Hair, Rhodochrosite, Star Hollandite, Tanzanite and Zebra Stone are good for anxiety in general. Apophyllite is excellent for when you cannot tolerate uncertainty and Beryl for when you're prone to mental over-analysis. Iron Pyrite overcomes a feeling of mental servitude and Rose Quartz calms mental agitation.*
- Boosting confidence: *Carnelian, Chrysocolla, Citrine, Dumortierite, Eudialyte, Eye of the Storm, Hematite, Iron Pyrite, Lazulite and Purpurite.*
- Boosting self-esteem: *Strawberry Quartz.*
- Boosting strength: *Bloodstone, Eye of the Storm, Flint, Jasper, Mahogany Obsidian, Merlinite, Obsidian, Onyx, Preseli Bluestone, Purpurite.*
- Breaking old patterns: *Brandenburg, Fenster or Phantom Quartz, Honey Calcite.*
- Letting go: *Azurite, Fenster Quartz, Fire Opal,*

Fulgarite, Nuummite, Paraiba Tourmaline, Rainbow Obsidian and Rutilated Quartz/Angel Hair. Garnet changes outworn ideas, Green Calcite moves stagnant energy or situations, Pumice lets go of feelings of vulnerability and Snow Quartz helps when you are weighed down by overwhelming responsibilities. Rainbow Mayanite aids release.

- Letting go of worrying what others think of you: *Pink Crackle Quartz.*
- Mid-life crisis: *Rose Quartz will steer you through a mid-life crisis, enabling you to get your life back on track or find the right pathway forward.*
- Neurosis: *Green Aventurine is beneficial in severe neurosis, helping you to understand what lies behind the condition.*
- Panic attacks: *Amethyst and Sodalite calm panic attacks. Keep a crystal in your pocket and hold it over your chest at the first sign of an attack. Breathe slowly and deeply and count to seven, hold the breath for a count of six and breathe out for a count of ten.*
- Phobias: *Sodalite is an excellent stone to help overcome phobias, whilst Green Aventurine specifically overcomes claustrophobia.*
- Psychiatric conditions: *An effective balancer of mood and a natural tranquillizer, Amethyst can assist in stabilizing psychiatric conditions. This powerful healing stone is extremely calming for your mind, helping you to feel less scattered. It should not, however, be used*

for the treatment of paranoia or schizophrenia.

- Reducing mental stress: *Amber, Beryl, Eye of the Storm, Laser Quartz, Spirit Quartz.*
- Rigid mental conditioning: *Agate or Sodalite gently releases old mental conditioning and dissolves a rigid mindset, allowing you to be more yourself.*
- An overly sensitive or defensive personality: *Sodalite releases the core fears and control mechanisms that underlie this problem and enhances self-acceptance.*
- Suicidal tendencies: *The gently cleansing and protective energies of Smoky Quartz or Eye of the Storm are excellent for alleviating suicidal urges, as they resolve any ambivalence about being in incarnation.*

CRYSTALS FOR HEALING DEPRESSION

An extremely debilitating mental state that may well have underlying emotional toxicity, depression manifests somewhat differently according to its cause but inevitably leaves you energetically depleted and vulnerable.

Reactive depression is a response to life events and is usually triggered by stressful personal situations or your family, but it may also be linked to emotional blockages or suppressed memories and is common in the partners of people who suffer from chronic depression. Reactive depression is alleviated by happy events or by the removal of the stressful situation. Typically, symptoms are less noticeable in the morning and increase during the day.

Endogenous depression is not alleviated by happy events

and is believed to be caused by biochemical imbalances, although emotional factors or spiritual dis-ease are also present. With this type of depression, there are disturbed sleep and eating patterns and a tendency to wake up feeling low.

Whilst approaches such as Cognitive Behavioural Therapy, EFT and counselling may well relieve the underlying causes of depression and teach how to handle its manifestations, and journalling can also reveal the hidden forces at work, carrying crystals can also be extremely helpful, particularly as a first-aid measure. Crystals such as Kunzite contain natural lithium – prescribed by the medical profession to regulate bipolar disorder.

Crystal Tips for Depression

- Labradorite *benefits reactive depression and steers you through necessary change into a place of calm.*
- Smoky Quartz *is useful for endogenous depression and alleviates suicidal tendencies. This stone gently dissolves any negative emotions or emotional blockages that underlie depression.*

Try This: Layout for Alleviating Depression

- Lie comfortably on your bed or on the floor. Ensure you won't be disturbed.
- Place an Amethyst on your brow to balance out emotional highs and lows and to promote emotional centring.
- Place Rose Quartz or Green Aventurine over

your heart to release unexpressed emotions and heartache, soothe your emotional pain and open your heart to unconditional love.

- Place Labradorite, Sunstone, Eye of the Storm or Smoky Quartz on your solar plexus to draw out fear and negative emotions, encourage you to let go of anything that no longer serves you and instil positive vibes in its place.
- Place Orange Carnelian on your sacral chakra to stabilize and anchor yourself into the present. Feel the vibrant energy of the stone radiating up through your whole body and down into the sexual chakras to gently transmute abuse of any kind. Be aware of the activation of your body's natural ability to heal and rebalance itself.
- Leave the stones in place for 15 to 20 minutes, then remove them and sit up slowly.
- Cleanse them thoroughly.

Additional Tools

Journalling (*Tool 6, page 19*), Crystal EFT (*Tool 27, page 65*), Gem Essences (*Tool 5, page 18*).

NEUTRALIZING THE ATTACKERS, WHOEVER THEY ARE

Dion Fortune's book *Psychic Self-Defence* was written in the main to explain how to safeguard yourself against what she called 'paranormal malevolence' from experienced practitioners of occultism and to explore the psychic reasons that can underlie mental illnesses. In other words, she was dealing with the magical and psychiatric realms rather than the everyday. If that is the kind of attack you find yourself under, reading her book or enlisting the assistance of a highly experienced practitioner may be required. But if you find yourself experiencing the more banal but nonetheless lethal everyday ill-wishing, psychic mugging or psychic attack, you'll find techniques and crystals here that will neutralize the attack. You'll also be able to discover how you unwittingly attack yourself and others and what you can do to reverse this.

PSYCHIC MUGGING

Psychic mugging is somewhat different from ill-wishing or psychic attack. It is usually not directly targeted at you, as it tends to happen when you step into the negative energy someone has left behind. Alternatively, there may be a 'once only' attack that comes from a hurtful remark, envious thought or malicious taunt. However, someone may psychically mug you in order to manipulate you or for reasons that appear to be benevolent. People going for psychic readings who are given 'bad news' in a tactless or too-direct way are being psychically mugged. Unwise psychics may say, 'I see a death,' and psychically sock their client in the solar plexus. Yet, as all psychics know, it is impossible to tell whether seeing a death means seeing the physical death of someone connected with you or the ending of something. So, choose your psychic reader with care.

Healing Psychic Mugging

This technique uses Tugtupite, a rare and expensive heart protector from Greenland, but Rose Quartz, Eudialyte or Rhodochrosite would be equally effective. It was the first-aid measure invented specially for the guy at Glastonbury who was psychically mugged, but you can use it whenever anything slams into your heart.

• Hold a piece of cleansed* Tugtupite over your higher heart chakra, in the centre of your chest a hand's breadth or so below your collarbone.

• Ask it to dissolve the pain and anything that may have been attached to the blow to your heart and to replace it with unconditional loving energy.

• Keep the stone in place until your heart feels eased and ask it to close the auric hole before you remove it.

Crystal Tips for Psychic Mugging to the Solar Plexus
Brandenberg; Elestial Quartz; Eudialyte; Green Ridge Quartz; Lemurian; Mangano Calcite; Rhodozaz; Rose or Smoky Quartz.

* Tugtupite is best cleansed with Petaltone Clear2Light or other crystal cleanser. Don't place it in water or use salt or it will disintegrate.

Mugging by Thought

I was given a graphic lesson in mugging by thought many years ago when I was trying, as a lone parent, to deal with an obstreperous teenager. A therapist encouraged me to picture my daughter and say to her everything that I was bottling up – all my frustrations, my fears for her and how they were affecting my life. There was no suggestion of forgiveness or reconciliation at the end of the session, which left me emotionally wrung out. But worse was to come when I reached home and found my daughter prostrate with a migraine. All those angry thoughts had clearly slammed right into her. Whilst that kind of emotional release can be useful, it needs to be as part of an ongoing process such as EFT or tie-cutting which emphasizes the healing, reconciliation, forgiveness and unconditional-love aspect of the process and it is sensible to protect the person concerned with a bubble of light (*Tool 7, page 20*) before you start.

ILL-WISHING AND PSYCHIC ATTACK

Ill-wishing tends to arise from short-term thoughts such as *I'll make him pay for that, I'll show her, Why didn't I get that job, I'm just as good as she is?* or *Why should he be so lucky?* especially when such thoughts are dwelt upon constantly. It can, however, happen just the once when negative thought slams into you, whether deliberately sent or not.

Psychic attack, which is more serious, is ongoing and arises from other people chewing over their resentments or deliberately directing malicious thoughts or energy your way. (To deal with prolonged psychic attack, see the protective measures in my book *Good Vibrations*.)

Most cases of ill-wishing or psychic attack usually occur through jealousy, envy, covetousness, grievance and anger, or a sense of injury or injustice, and most are unconscious. That is, they aren't deliberately targeted. The attack arises out of repressed or unnoticed feelings or the envious or vengeful thoughts people turn over in their mind, or the litany of criticism they vent without realizing the damage they cause.

However, there is another, more subtle, form of ill-wishing that can arise from a seemingly benevolent activity. This occurs when allegedly well-meaning friends discuss another friend behind their back. They may be discussing that friend 'for their own good', pointing out 'defects' and how these could be remedied, but so often it turns into a slagging-off. They may even then tell the person concerned. I find it often occurs when supposedly spiritual people feel that they have reached a higher level of understanding than the people around them and begin to discuss how their friends 'don't get it'. They don't even need to mention it to the person concerned because simply having the thought can do damage. This spiritual elitism can be experienced in the form of an attack that may bring up a person's deepest fears and emotions. So, the feeling of 'being got at', judged to be inferior, not getting it right again and so on can arise in the 'friend'. EFT tapping works extremely well for removing this result, but it would be better if the source – the gossip, no matter how spiritually or benevolently packaged – were removed at source.

Psychic attack can also arise out of a need to dominate and be right. Parents and teachers psychically attack children by telling them how useless they are and bullies and the power hungry pick on those weaker than themselves. It's not always that obvious: sexual harassment is just as much a form of psychic attack, as is religious fanaticism or the constant bombardment of information about global warming, your carbon footprint and the like. It all creates a state of vulnerability.

It has been brought to my attention again recently that if you are well protected and come under ill-wishing or psychic attack, the effect can roll off you but land on vulnerable people around you or your computer or car. I had once again come under attack from someone who had jealousy issues to work on. I am well protected, but was aware that somewhere in the distance something was trying to get through and it looked like a rearing cobra, an energy that I didn't want anywhere near me. As I don't like turning psychic attack back onto the person concerned, because that only amps it up until it becomes a psychic battle, I thought it would be enough to protect myself and vulnerable people around me and put some 'cotton wool' into the ether to mop up what was being sent out. Unfortunately, I underestimated the force of the animosity and overlooked putting something in place to transmute it. For the first time ever, and despite having recently upgraded my anti-virus software, my computer was invaded by a 'rather nasty little worm', as my computer guy put it. My computer is usually also protected by the amazing Computer Clear program, which picks up things like psychic attack and neutralizes them, but that was awaiting reactivation, so the computer was more vulnerable than usual.

At the same time the light in my fridge blew, always a sign in my house that all is not well energetically.

But this was not all. A friend, who was going through a tough time of her own and was particularly emotionally vulnerable, asked me to follow her in my car while she went to collect something in hers, in case she needed back-up. Her car happens to be my old car and was, or so I thought, well protected, as was she. But as I followed her I was aware of a horrible burning smell and the odd bit of smoke. I flashed her, but she blithely went on her way, so I assumed, wrongly as it turned out, that all was well. Suddenly, half a mile from our destination, she pulled off the road into a convenient layby (the only one on that road) and said, 'I can't change gear.' The clutch had blown. Now the car is old and I'd done rather a lot of miles on that clutch as I'd had the car from new, so it may well have been coincidence, but it felt like synchronicity – events in the outer world mirroring those in the inner for my friend who was striving to change gear in her life – as well as a part of the attack I was under. What was useful was that we were in the only spot for quite a distance where a mobile phone actually worked, so we were able to get the AA in quickly and the guy took her home after dropping off her car at the garage. As the person she was collecting from lived very close by, he was able to bring what she needed to her before the AA arrived.

When I got home I called a healer/dowser who helps me out with protection when necessary and he confirmed that the incidents were a result of 'spillage' from the lethal attack hitting something vulnerable when it couldn't get to me: the computer, a light bulb and the old worn-out clutch. Although financially inconvenienced, my friend and I were unharmed. It would, however, have been useful to have extended the protection to cover 'incidentals'.

To counteract the possibility of 'spillage', keep those you love and your car well protected with pink light or a suitably programmed Black Tourmaline, Shungite or Rainbow Obsidian, ensure that the virus checker on your computer is always up to date and use Psychic Shields (*Tool 18, page 47*) if necessary. If you know the source of attack, mentally picturing a big vacuum cleaner in front of the person that sends the energy deep into space for transmutation can also help, as can transmutation crystals such as Black Tourmaline, Nuummite, Smoky Quartz and Shungite, suitably programmed to both mop up and transmute the energy.

How Do You Recognize an Attack?

There are many ways in which you can recognize you are under attack or ill-wishing – you may have been told by someone that you are, for instance – but some or all of the signs below will probably be present (although they can also be signs of stress or depression). But do keep a sense of proportion about this, because what you fear tends to manifest and there may be other reasons for the symptoms. A sudden and total loss of energy can signify a new attack or it could just indicate stress and overactive adrenal glands.

Signs of ill-wishing, psychic mugging or psychic attack:
- a sudden total energy drain
- debilitating fatigue
- a feeling of invasion
- a feeling of being watched
- being accident prone
- waking suddenly in the night feeling someone is there
- your life not working

- constant illness
- computers crashing or light bulbs blowing
- bodily pain – sudden and sharp or a continuous dull ache
- incessant negative thoughts that are somehow 'not yours'
- panic attacks
- nightmares
- a fear of being alone.

Ill-wishing or psychic attack can be more potent when you know someone has it in for you. This is because ill-wishing works most strongly through:
- fear
- the power of suggestion
- intention.

And psychic attack or ill-wishing is most effective when there is:
- knowledge of the intention
- energetic weakness
- loose boundaries
- belief.

Try This: Blocking Psychic Attack or Ill-wishing

Apart from wearing a Black Tourmaline, Tantalite or Shungite over your thymus, grid the corners of your house with these crystals and, if the attack is severe, your bed as well, and place one of them in your car, suitably programmed to protect you.

Treasure Chest

BLACK TOURMALINE

Black Tourmaline is the most effective block to psychic attack and an extremely efficient 'mopper-upper' of 'black' energy. Its inner lattice traps negative energy, especially electromagnetic energy, and prevents it from reaching you. It's excellent for blocking ill-wishing and emanations from mobile phones and for drawing off stress. Wear it over your thymus whenever you come under energetic attack of any kind. It helps you to adopt a laid-back positive attitude no matter what the circumstances.

POLYCHROME JASPER

Polychrome Jasper is an extremely efficient shield against ill-wishing and psychic attack, particularly as it is such a new find and therefore its energetic signature is unknown on the ether. It balances the physical and subtle bodies and provides grounding and stability. This 'stone of happiness' helps you to tread a new pathway and to find fresh joy in your life.

Additional Tools

Amulets (*Tool 3, page 15*), Guardian Angels (*Tool 17, page 44*), Psychic Shields (*Tool 18, page 47*).

THE POWER OF BELIEF

Forty years ago I lived in Sierra Leone, where the power of the 'juju man' (witch doctor) was legendary. Although the people were nominally Christian or Muslim (depending on which missionary school had been attended), deep in the bush where I was living all the old customs were carried on and we were close to a forbidden village, Imabu, home of the juju man, at which we would gaze with awe from the other side of the river, having read a graphic account by the wife of the former manager of the mine, one of the first visitors to the region, of how the juju men turned sticks into snakes and put the evil eye on those who angered them. The mental scene was set by that fascinating account and the emotional one by feeling the emanations of that mysterious and somehow malevolent village across the water with its round huts and the befeathered and painted young natives who occasionally came and shook their fists at us. Like teenagers everywhere, they were keen to mark their territory and we would frequently come across 'fetishes' – keep-out signs – planted by the side of the road. The juju men were past masters at creating a climate of fear.

Even in the capital, Freetown, the juju man was a force to be reckoned with. When I first arrived and was waiting at the airport to go up country, I was shown a heap of twisted metal and a brand new hangar a few yards to the side of it. A smiling face said, 'Big white boss man he be building hangar here. We tell him it juju spirit path, he no take notice. He build it, it fall down. He building it again, it fall down. He building it again! He building it – over there.'

Even though the mine at which I lived provided work for local people, the juju man did not approve and cursed the dredge, which promptly turned turtle and sank. His magic was seen as mighty indeed.

Local people turned up at the mine surgery with inexplicable illnesses after being cursed by the juju man. The American nurse who treated them had lived in the bush for over 50 years and was most respectful of the juju. She would say, 'Once the bone has been pointed, it's done.' Several of the cursed people died.

Then we had a new doctor, one who had worked in the Solomon Islands in the Pacific, which had a similar culture. When he arrived he told everyone his medicine was more powerful than that of the juju man and he waved a large hypodermic horse syringe around to prove it. There were no more deaths from mystery illness amongst the locals, although the mine had many misfortunes and the curse had repercussions for many years until it was lifted.[9] The mining was for Rutile and the rock contained large deposits of Amethyst – both excellent psychic protectors if only I'd consciously known how to use them at the time, although I still have a piece of Rutile crystal I picked up in my African garden and it's beside my bed – now thoroughly cleansed, of course.

One of the things I learned from my stay in Africa was how objects such as masks or statues can be imbued with malevolent energy – often done as a way of protecting them from theft. Dion Fortune talks in her book about Buddha figures that, whilst outwardly beneficial, had been imbued with less than helpful magical energy by some of the darker sects of Tibetan Buddhism. If you have such objects and are doubtful of their benevolent intent, have them checked out and cleansed thoroughly by someone who is trained in magical protection techniques, or send them back to where they belong. In an emergency, Z14 will clear them.

However, keep in mind that the power of belief can also be used to good effect to change your present and your future. If you believe something strongly enough and focus all your intention and attention on it, then you can bring it into being. So, if you believe that you are totally and fully protected, you are.

Not Only Baddies Attack

Psychic attack doesn't only occur when the 'baddies' become angry. Even the so-called 'good' can use psychic attack to get what they want, especially if they feel it's owed to them or is sanctioned by their god. The Old Testament story of Moses and Aaron graphically portrays the ancient world of magic and illustrates how psychic attack works no matter what the culture:

> 'Moses and Aaron did as the Lord had commanded.
> [Aaron] lifted up his staff and struck the water of the Nile
> and all the water was changed into blood. The fish died
> and the river stank... Aaron stretched out his hand over the
> waters of Egypt, and the frogs came up and covered the
> land... Aaron stretched out his staff and struck the dust, and
> it turned into maggots on man and beast... swarms of flies...
> all the herds of Egypt died... festering boils [affected] men
> and beasts... violent hailstorms... thunder and fire... locusts...
> darkness over the land of Egypt... and every firstborn son
> of Egypt died.'   Exodus 4–12

All this so that the Pharaoh would be forced to let the Israelites leave Egypt.

Not all psychic attack produces plagues and death, but it can be extremely detrimental to your health until you learn to block it. The Pharaoh and the people of Egypt would undoubtedly have benefited from Black Tourmaline around their necks, but that stone doesn't seem to have been in their magical repertoire, although plenty of others were.

It may surprise you to know that much of the ill-wishing and many of the psychic attacks people experience don't come from other people at all, but from their own negative thoughts and toxic emotions that are projected out onto the world and rebound as though coming from an outside source. It's as though you psychically mug yourself.

By now you should be able to catch yourself when you start to run the kind of negative mental programme or the toxic emotional expectations that create self-attack by thoughts such as 'I'm not good enough' or 'I'll never be able to do that' or beliefs such as 'It always happens to me,' 'I'm always the one who's cheated/betrayed/etc.' and so on.

By now you have hopefully learned to shut it off at source, but if not, try journalling (*Tool 6, page 19*), affirmations (*Tool 13, page 36*), positive thought (*Tool 16, page 42*), psychic shields (*Tool 18, page 47*), believing in yourself (*Tool 24, page 58*) or EFT (*Tool 27, page 65*). And remember to keep control of your thoughts so that you don't inadvertently attack someone else.

DEALING WITH PSYCHIC ATTACK

But what do you do when you, inadvertently or otherwise, upset someone else enough for them to ill-wish or even psychically attack you, consciously or otherwise? Well, the fastest way to block such energies is to wear a Black Tourmaline over your thymus. The next thing is quietly to repeat to yourself: 'I'm sorry, I love you, please forgive me.' You're not saying this to the other person – after all, psychic attack is often anonymous and you may not even know the source – but rather just putting the energy of love and forgiveness out there on the ether.

Dealing with Psychic Attack from a Known Source

If you do know the source, try the following:

- Put yourself in a light bubble and wear Black Tourmaline, Shungite, Polychrome Jasper, Tantalite or Master Shamanite.
- Invoke your angel of protection and any religious figure you find helpful.
- Disconnect from the person – remove yourself from their space and their energy – physically, emotionally, mentally and spiritually.
- Laugh about it to yourself – don't take it too seriously or give it too much energy.
- Take your attention away from it and onto something positive.
- Don't play the other person's game or get pulled into power struggles.
- Don't see them, speak or think about them.

- Don't meditate or open yourself up psychically.
- Avoid drugs, alcohol or consciousness-altering substances.
- If you have to, face up to the person fearlessly, keeping your boundaries strong.

If necessary you can put up a mental mirror to return the ill-will to its source, but this tends to perpetuate it and it may be better to ask your angel of protection to absorb and transmute the energy instead.

Many people suggest sending love in this situation. I don't, because I've had too many personal experiences of doing so and then having the love taken up and used to fuel a further onslaught – the person picking up on the love seeing it as vulnerability and a way in. There are times when unconditional love does not overcome hate, and psychic attack is one of them. Forgiveness, on the other hand, can help, although this may need to be done at a later stage. The best path of all is to withdraw your attention, find joy in living and leave whoever it is to get on with it. They'll soon tire of a game they have to play alone with no rewards.

When Love Turns to Hate

One of the most prevalent sources of psychic attack is when a relationship – no matter what kind – ends. Many people unwittingly use their child as a weapon in the battle, but inanimate objects can also take on this role, as I found when I sat in the back of a car that had been cursed by a powerful shaman with whom the owner had fallen out after finding she wasn't the only person having a sexual relationship with him. The woman who owned the car was well protected, but the back seat was not and I could feel it all around me. Having cleaned my own energies, I thoroughly sprayed the car with Ti essence to lift the curse and Z14 and Clear2Light to clear the last remnants of the shaman's energy. My client used Ti herself, dispersed into her aura, together with the Z14 and Clear2Light essences. We carried out a tie-cutting with the shaman and smudged her thoroughly. We protected the car with a grid of Black Tourmaline and Labradorite and Selenite to bring in spiritual protection energies. She then had to take the drum she had bought from the shaman, beat it thoroughly to reclaim her power, and then set fire to it in her garden, as she realized it was also imbued with the curse.

Not everyone has to take such drastic action, but psychic attack is something to take seriously if it comes from an external source and not from within your own self – which is equally serious but can be dealt with in a completely different way by identifying your inner terrorist (*see page 194*).

Gridding and Rebounding

Gridding is an excellent way to ward off psychic attack or ill-wishing (*see Tool 2, Crystal layouts, page 14*) but you need to choose your stones with care. Bronzite and Black Tourmaline are both sold as protectors against psychic attack, but there is a subtle difference: Black Tourmaline absorbs the attack, while Bronzite turns it back to its source. Although the person putting out the attack feels the effects as it rebounds, they may not be aware of putting out the attack and may become defensive or aggressive in turn. So the attack bounces backwards and forwards, becoming more and more hyped up. To counteract this effect, place three Bronzites in a downward-pointing triangle and over the top place three upward-pointing Black Tourmalines to form a hexagram, as this absorbs and blocks the attack, preventing a rebound. Bronzite is, however, an excellent stone for creating a calm safe space in which to meditate or vision.

Note that Crystal Balance Detachment Spray is excellent for separating energies between ex-partners.

Treasure Chest

PERIDOT

Peridot is an extremely helpful stone for anyone with a jealous nature, as it alleviates jealousy, resentment, spitefulness and anger and reduces stress. It also enhances confidence, assists in looking back to the past to find the gift in your experiences and shows how to forgive yourself and how to let go of feeling that other people have what you want or are living the life you want. A clear emerald green, it is often set into rings or pendants and should be worn daily.

MASTER SHAMANITE

A black Calcite sold as a journeying tool, Master Shamanite is also extremely helpful in cases of psychic attack as it soaks up and neutralizes the attack. It works particularly well in tandem with Tantalite.

JOURNALLING FOR INNER COMMUNICATION

If you've been keeping a journal of your fears and experiences you may well find certain mental patterns or obsessive thoughts have emerged that are actually a form of personal psychic mugging or attack that can be turned around by using re-visioning or affirmations and positive thought (*see Tools 14 and 16, pages 37 and 42*). You can take this a stage further by using your journal to communicate with figures who people your inner world and who may well be contributing to your psychic vulnerability without your awareness.

Try This: 'Are You There?'

• Take a new page in your journal and, focusing your attention deep into yourself and keeping your bubble of light firmly around you to ensure it's only your inner world with which you communicate, write the question: 'Is there anybody in my inner world who wants to communicate with me?'

• Wait quietly and write down any answer you receive. If possible, get a dialogue going with this figure. Ask what it represents, what it does, what messages it has for you. You may find it's your own picture of someone from your past, or one of your own memories, or ingrained conditioning, or perhaps a deceased relative is hanging on (*in which case, see page 122 and release them*).

• Allow whatever wants to come, don't censor it, and gradually ask, 'What is the positive side of

this? Is there anything I can do for you? How can
we work together for my well-being?'

- Repeat the exercise over a few days and see what
changes. If you need to re-vision and change
scenarios and thought patterns, use the tools in
Part I to assist you.

Finding the Inner Terrorist

As ill-wishing and psychic attack can arise from your own
inner self, a visioning exercise can help you to identify
whether there is an inner terrorist living within you and
psychically mugging you, and to negotiate any changes
necessary. This exercise can be adapted to find other
destructive inner figures, too, such as an inner critic, judge
or control freak. Carrying a Super 7 or Scapolite crystal
can assist.

Try This: Meeting the Inner Terrorist

- Sit quietly and let yourself relax. Picture in your
mind an ancient fortress perched on a hill with a
path leading up to it.
- Let your feet take you over to this fortress.
See how strongly it was built and notice whether
it's now ruined or has breaches in its defences.
Enter it and explore.
- When you're ready to seek the inner terrorist,
look down at your feet. You'll see a trap door
there. Open this trap door and descend the
ladder below. Remember to take a light with you
or look for a light switch as you go down the
ladder.

- Look around you. This is where your inner terrorist lives. This figure may be reluctant to come out into the light and may prefer to stay in a dark corner. If this is the case, try to reassure it and coax it into the light so you can communicate more easily.
- Look at the figure, see how it's dressed, what era it stems from and what its manner is (it may not show itself as human).
- Ask the figure what purpose it serves and what hidden parts of you it represents. Wait quietly and patiently for the answer – don't push. Listen compassionately and don't try to make excuses for anything that may be said. You'll probably find the figure once had a positive purpose but this has changed over the years. If so, thank it for its care and concern, explain that things are different now and let the terrorist feel your love, forgiveness and compassion enfolding it.
- Ask the terrorist if it will help you by taking a more positive role in your inner life.
- If the answer is 'yes', discuss this and ask for a new name to go with its new role. If the answer is 'no', ask the terrorist if it's willing to leave you and take up residence somewhere where it won't frustrate your purpose. You may need to do some negotiating here. Most terrorists eventually agree to become more positive or to leave.
- Occasionally an inner terrorist is merely a thought form you've internalized. If so, ask your guardian angel to help you dissolve it.
- If your terrorist absolutely refuses to change, you may need a different approach under the

guidance of someone qualified in dispossession techniques (*see page 124 for emergency advice and* Good Vibrations *for further assistance*). In the meantime, wrap the terrorist in a light bubble and send it back to where you initially found it.

- When you've completed your discussions or negotiations, leave by the ladder and close the trap door. The figure may well come with you and can be encouraged to find an appropriate place to settle or to leave for good.

- When you're ready, open your eyes. Take your attention down to your feet and feel them standing on the Earth. Picture a shield closing over your third eye and a light bubble surrounding you. With your eyes wide open, take a deep breath and stand up with your feet firmly on the Earth, grounding you.

- Record the experience in your journal and remember to transmute any negative thoughts and emotions the terrorist revealed into positive thoughts or affirmations.

Crystals Tips for Overcoming Self-sabotage and Inner Terrorism

Larimar, Scapolite, Tourmalinated Quartz, Super 7, Turquoise.

Crystals Tips for Overcoming Inner Criticism

Aventurine, Blue Chalcedony, Rainbow Obsidian, Rose Quartz, Rutilated Quartz.

Attack from Beyond

Not all psychic attack comes from those in the here and now – some 'ghosts' can be extremely active in their dislike of the living, for what they think is a good reason but is usually seriously outdated. On the estate where I used to live, for example, there was an almshouse that no one could sleep in. As soon as a person tried to sleep there, they'd be shaken awake by a voice saying, 'Get out of my bed, I won't have you here,' followed by poking and prodding. The old man who lived in the almshouse – and who'd had to resort to sleeping in a chair in his sitting room – was quite psychic and could see 'a shadow' but couldn't get any information from it, so asked me to take a look.

Talking to the spirit elicited that the voice belonged to a woman who had lived in that house for a very long time, so long in fact that she'd forgotten exactly when she had moved in. As the almshouses dated back to 1647, it was quite possible she'd been there for 400 years or so. Time makes little difference to these beings. The first thing I had to do was divert a ley line that ran through the bedroom and that was assisting her in staying put. Then I settled down for a long talk with her and finally convinced her that she could move on. She went willingly to the light, where her husband was patiently waiting.

It would have been useful to have had Z14 to assist as, since the old man died, people have rarely stayed in that particular house for long, usually because there has been 'something' in the bedroom. I don't think it's that woman, but it may be an energy imprint (which many ghosts are) or it may be that the energy line has moved back. Either way, without being invited, it's not possible for me to do any more.

E-mail Attack

I really can't finish this section without mentioning those awful circular e-mails that fill my inbox because 'friends' who are at a loss to fill their quota of passing them on within the next ten minutes tend to think of me first, despite my telling them I instantly delete them without opening them, so any benefits they hope to accrue are lost. These e-mails are the equivalent of the old poison-pen chain letters. Many are, on the surface, beneficent and promise many blessings if you send them on to dozens of your friends. Others are more direct in their promise of divine retribution if you ignore them. All are a subtle form of psychic attack and can safely be sent to the great recycling bin in the sky and instantly forgotten about. If you let fear intervene and begin to wonder whether something bad will happen if you ignore them, you can be sure it will! So let them go with love and forgiveness and leave the great god Cyberspace to sort it out.

If you are really concerned, programme a crystal to protect you (*see page 12*). Eye of the Storm is particularly effective.

PROTECTING FAMILY AND FRIENDS

In terms of protecting others, it isn't enough simply to change your attitude about yourself; if you're fearful for others, it has the same insidious effect on them as fearing for yourself does. So, while you cannot keep other people totally protected, you can play your part by picturing them safe, happy and well, and safely wrapped up in pink light – and by encouraging them to use the techniques in this book.

All of the techniques in this book *can* be applied to other people, but it is better if they do them for themselves, so please share the book as widely as possible.

Try This

Whenever you are concerned about someone's safety or well-being, picture them surrounded by pink light. This is not your light, it is their light, perhaps supplied by their guardian angel or their higher self, but definitely theirs and not yours. So then take your attention away and let the light do its work.

PROTECTING CHILDREN

Children may well appear to be unable to protect themselves, especially from the thoughts and feelings of the adults around them, but it's amazing how resilient they are and how creative. Many children find their own ways of psychically protecting themselves without any assistance from adults. They have to for their own sanity sometimes. Almost every child has a safe place into which they withdraw and a protector on whom they call, even if this is unknown to the adults around them. Being highly intuitive, they are often aware of 'ghosts' and may well have spirit friends who won't harm them and indeed are often there for protection.

One of the best ways to protect children is to ensure you're absolutely honest and open, never thinking one thing but saying another. Don't harbour anger and resentment and deny it, as children are aware of such conflicts and it confuses them, as does a bad atmosphere or a huge amount of unspoken anger into which they unknowingly walk – exactly like a psychic mugging.

If you feel a child needs protection, you can visualize them surrounded by bright white or pink light and ask their angel of protection to be with them – or do the angel of protection exercise with the child, as it shows them from a young age how to be protected. Children also like the jumping into a shiny new dustbin or wearing a spacesuit types of protection, although many also go for the pyramid and the bubble of light.

Most children are attracted to crystals and like to wear a 'shaman's pouch' of protective crystals – kept cleansed, of course – or have a crystal or two in their pocket or under their pillow. However, the best protection of all for your children is to monitor your own thoughts and feelings and teach them to do the same for themselves from an early age without any feelings being labelled 'bad' but with an awareness of the consequences of negative thoughts and toxic emotions.

Additional Tools
Psychic Shields (*Tool 8, page 47*), Animal Allies (*Tool 26, page 61*), Gem Essences (*Tool 5, page 18*).

FAMILY BREAK-UP

Children are often the ones who suffer most when a family breaks up, especially when they are used as weapons by one of the adults against the other – yet another subtle form of psychic attack or psychic mugging.

Andrew's case history shows clearly our psychic energy is not 'all of a piece' but can fragment and scatter, especially when loyalties are torn. He came to me because his energy was being severely drained and he wanted to etherically clear the ties with his ex-wife after an acrimonious divorce that had taken several years to complete. After the tie-cutting, I could still see a small child. When I checked it out, I found that Andrew was not allowed access to his daughter, as her mother had been using her as a weapon, but he had a strong connection with her that the daughter was desperate to keep. Even though she was older now, part of her psychic energy was with her father as the small child she had been when her mother had taken her away. In a visioning exercise, Andrew was able to show his daughter what had happened and how to reintegrate the energy and he promised he would find a way for them to be together physically. He did indeed find a way to break the deadlock about access and his daughter became whole once more.

Now that, like Andrew, you've taken a good look at what's tripped you up in life or what may lie behind unpleasant experiences, it's time to put your thoughts, attention and intention onto the positive side and attract some beneficial vibes into your life.

PART III
ACCENTUATE
THE POSITIVE

Accentuate the Positive

'Like attracts like.'

Esoteric dictum

In this part of the book we are going to look at things you can do to increase your positivity, which keeps your energy high and provides natural protection.

We will begin by attending to your spiritual health and your connection with something greater than yourself. This helps you to be more positive and centred in your emotional and mental life.

One thing to remember, though, is not to expect to do it all at once. Break things down into manageable and easily achievable chunks. Set goals and targets rather than expectations. Take one step at a time and stay in the present moment rather than galloping ahead of yourself. Remember that where you are right now is where you're meant to be. If you can learn to accept that and can be in the present moment without needing to change it, without needing to do anything in fact, you're well on the way to natural self-protection.

FINDING INNER PEACE

Inner peace is perhaps the most vital tool of all. If you feel safe within yourself, centred within a calm space around an unshakeable central core, and well grounded, no matter what is going on externally you'll always feel protected. You'll find the exercises that follow invaluable for creating instant inner peace.

THE AMBER MELT

This exercise is a variation on Tool 7, the Bubble of Light. Due to the qualities of Amber, it creates a safe space around and within you in which fears simply dissolve and peace takes over.

Treasure Chest

AMBER

Strictly speaking, Amber is a solidified tree resin rather than a crystal, but it has been used for adornment and protection for over 45,000 years. A useful grounding stone, it creates a protective barrier, cleanses negative energy and fearful thoughts, rebalances them with inner peace, brings stability and promotes a positive mental attitude.

Treasure Chest

GALAXYITE

Galaxyite's extremely high vibrations connects you to the entire cosmos, helping you understand the immensity of creation. It provides auric protection during all metaphysical work and simultaneously keeps you grounded and expanded. Journeying with this stone takes you to the far reaches of our universe and beyond. Expanding consciousness, Galaxyite helps take an overview on your lives and your spiritual development, attuning you to your soul purpose.

Try This

- Close your eyes, breathe gently and hold a piece of Amber over your head (or place it at your head if you're lying down). Put all your attention into the crystal.
- Feel the Amber slowly melting and trickling like honey all around your energy field until it completely coats it, meeting under your feet.
- Feel how safe it is within your Amber cloak, how secure, and how easily you can find your centre and grounding within this beautiful crystal.
- Allow the crystal to draw off and transmute any negative energy or fearful emotions, de-stressing you and filling you with positive self-regard and inner peace.
- Feel how, from the top of your head down into your heart, and on down to the earth beneath your feet, you have a central core of deep peace you can lean and rely on.

- When you're ready to end, withdraw your attention from the crystal but leave your bubble in place so that when you return your attention into the room you'll still have that core of inner peace. Stamp your foot to close down and ground yourself into the everyday once more.

If you carry your piece of Amber with you throughout the day, once you've established the Amber bubble, simply touching the stone will recreate it and reassure you that you have inner peace at any time. Alternatively, you can place your Amber over your heart on the vision board you created as Tool 19.

Alternative Crystal
The new Eye of the Storm crystal creates a peaceful centre deep within and all around you. You can use it as an alternative to Amber, holding it to your heart and taking the peace deep within and all around you.

Additional Tools
Relaxation Crystals (*Tool 4, page 17*), Journalling (*Tool 6, page 19*), Breathing (*Tool 9, page 25*), Getting Grounded (*Tool 10, page 28*), Trust (*Tool 12, page 34*), Gratitude and Blessing (*Tool 23, page 56*) and Happiness (*Tool 25, page 59*), also meditation (*see page 217*).

FINDING SERENITY

Inner serenity equals inner peace. If you're able to be in a place of inner serenity, nothing can rock your equilibrium. In the following journey you'll travel into a place of profound peace, the inner temple of your own heart, and bring that serenity back into everyday life. If you carry a crystal with you it will always remind you of your safe, serene place.

Treasure Chest

COVELLITE

Attuned to your highest self, Covellite supports intention and assists if you're feeling vulnerable or too easily influenced by others. This metallic stone overcomes discontent and replaces it with contentment. It facilitates loving yourself unconditionally and releases anything holding you back, replacing negative emotions with loving serenity.

Try This: The Temple of the Heart

Settle yourself quietly, holding a crystal if you wish.

- Close your eyes and breathe gently, withdrawing your attention from the outside world. Focus your attention on your heartbeat, feeling it in your chest and hearing the beat with your inner ear.

- As you listen to the beat, let it transport you on a journey to the temple of your heart. You may find this within your physical body or you may travel to the temple of the heart in another dimension. Simply let the heartbeat take you there. This is a place of profound love and deep inner peace. Let that peace and love settle into every pore of your being.
- As this peace pours into you, be aware of your connection with the spiritual world, with the divine love that emanates from the heart of the universe. Let this connection strengthen so you'll always be attuned to this love and can draw on it at any time. Fill your heart with this love and if you're holding a crystal, place this to your heart so that it, too, fills with love.
- When it's time to leave the temple of the heart, thank the divine energy for being with you and your own heart for being there for you and being a container for this love. Let the serenity of your heart guide you in the days to come. Let your heartbeat transport you back into awareness of your body.
- Bring your attention back into the room, stand up and stamp your feet to reground yourself.

Crystal Tips to Bring Serenity
Amethyst, Celestite, Covellite, Eye of the Storm,
Rhodochrosite, Rose Quartz, Selenite.

Crystal Tips for Centring Yourself
Agate (physical), Amethyst (emotional), Eye of the Storm,
Selenite or Pietersite (spiritual), Star Sapphire (mental).

MANIFEST THE SELF

If you are safely anchored in your true Self, the part of you that is only partially in incarnation – and which can see further and knows far more than the small self, which is connected to the ego – you'll feel totally secure and completely authentic.

To fully manifest your Self, rather than being influenced by others or trying to conform to the norm, hold a piece of lavender-blue Zoisite or wear Gaia Stone, Tanzanite or Tanzine Aura Quartz.

Treasure Chest

AMMOLITE

Ammolite is an ammonite fossil that has metamorphosized into an iridescent coating. Its whorls take you deep into yourself to find your true self or out into the universe to connect to your higher self. Representing coming full circle and knowing the place for the first time, it has the soul's path encoded within it. Ammolite stimulates survival instincts, showing that you get there if you persevere.

Try This: Manifesting the Self

• Settle yourself in a comfortable place and hold the crystal you've chosen to assist in manifesting your Self. Breathe gently and easily. Lift your

shoulders up to your ears, pull them back and let
go with a big sigh, letting go any tension you may
be feeling.

• Take your awareness to your heart and the higher
heart chakra located above it (*see page 107*);
you can touch them to focus your attention there.
Allow these chakras to unfold, opening like the
petals of a flower.

• Take your attention up to the crown chakra at the
top of your head. Allow this chakra to fully open.
The chakras above your head now also expand
and open and you may feel a string pulling
you up. Allow yourself to go with this feeling.
Consciously allow your vibrations to rise, to reach
the highest possible level.

• Invite your Self to move down through these
chakras until it fills your crown chakra. From the
crown chakra, feel your Self enfold your whole
body. Experience the love your Self has for you
and the wisdom it carries. Draw that love deep
into your being.

• Invite your Self to move into your heart and
ask that it manifests fully in your life. Feel how
protected you are, how your vibrations are raised
by the manifestation of your Self. Place your
crystal over your heart and invite your Self to
resonate with the crystal.

• When you are ready to end the exercise, ask
your Self to remain with you, safely within your
heart but continuing its expanded perception
and awareness. Gently close the chakras above
your head, letting them fold in on themselves like

flowers closing for the night. Close the crown and third eye chakras and make sure that your earth chakra is holding you firmly in incarnation. Slowly, bring your attention back to your physical body and the room around you. Check your grounding cord is in place and get up and move around.

• Whenever you need reminding to manifest your Self, hold your crystal to your heart.

Crystal Tips for Manifesting the Self

Ajoite, Bastnasite, Chrysotile in Serpentine, Flint, Nirvana Quartz, Prehnite with Epidote, Selenite, Sandstone, Spirit Quartz, Stitchite, Rainbow Mayanite, Tanzanite, Trigonic Quartz, Zoisite.

WHAT DOES MY BODY SAY?

Not only does your body language tell other people how you are feeling, and transmit fears or feelings of vulnerability over a wide distance to attract predators or manipulators, but it also affects how you yourself feel. If your body looks as though it's fearful, it probably is. But change your stance and you change the chemical messengers flying around your body that tell you how you feel.[10] If you can stand tall and confident, you'll feel confident and at peace with yourself.

Think about your body language for a moment. Looking in a mirror, especially catching sight of yourself when you aren't prepared for it, can be revealing. Ask yourself:

• 'Are my shoulders hunched?'
• 'Is one shoulder raised as though to ward off a blow?'

- 'Are my arms held tight across my chest?'
- 'Are my hands clenched into fists?'
- 'Do I have a defensive stance?'
- 'Am I standing on tiptoe ready to run?'
- 'Is my forehead puckered into a frown?'
- 'Do my eyes dart about, constantly monitoring my space?'
- 'Is my neck tense and hunkered down into my shoulders?'
- 'Are my shoulders tense?'
- 'Am I smiling, relaxed and standing tall, looking confident and serenely facing the world?'

If your stance is anything but the last, make changes now.

Treasure Chest

RED JASPER

Red Jasper is an excellent grounding and energizing stone. It nurtures you during stress, induces tranquillity and infuses you with life-force. It supports your determination, cleanses negative energy and blocks environmental pollution. If you've problems, this stone helps you to get to grips with the underlying causes of them. It supports you during necessary conflict or change. Place a piece of Red Jasper in your hip pocket to stimulate your creative juices and keep your base chakras energized, your pelvis moving freely and your walk confident.

Try This: The Confident Stance

- Straighten up and drop your shoulders, pulling them back and smiling as you do so.
- Take a deep breath and open up your solar plexus, pulling your arms back and up over your head before letting all your breath out with a big sigh as you drop your arms.
- Flap your hands about and shake your arms. Loosen up those wrists.
- Shake out your legs and wiggle your hips around.
- Stand tall, shoulders back, head up, eyes wide open and facing the front and arms loose by your sides.
- Smile inwardly and recall the happiest moment in your life.
- Practise walking with confident ease, head held high and eyes looking straight ahead.

Additional Tool

Make a vision board (*Tool 19, page 49*) of people who exude confidence and serenity. Put a variety of smiles and stances on the board. Practise them in front of a mirror until you, too, exude confidence.

Releasing your Pelvis

The base of the spine holds a great deal of tension and can affect how you hold yourself and how freely you move. It can also lock creative energy up tightly. If you release your pelvis, this energy can flow.

Treasure Chest

KEYIAPO

A mix of Iron Pyrite and Quartz, Keyiapo provides a protective shield while encouraging consciousness to reach the highest dimensions. It grounds energy into the body, spirit into matter and settles the soul deeper into incarnation, retaining a strong connection to the Higher Self. Keyiapo assists reading the Akashic Record and facilitates journeying to previous lives. It cleanses the auric bodies and the karmic blueprint, removing dis-ease and instilling a sense of well-being.

Try This: The Pelvic Swing

- Stand comfortably and loosely with your feet a couple of feet apart. Allow your knees to bend a little.
- Keeping your shoulders still, push your pelvis forwards and swing it to the left, then push it backwards and swing it to the right. Be aware that you are rotating around the calm peaceful centre of your being.
- Repeat 10 times and then reverse the direction. Your energy should be flowing freely.
- Now take your attention to the base of your spine and feel your connection with the Earth beneath your feet.

Additional Tools

Affirmations (*Tool 13, page 36*), Happiness (*Tool 25, page 59*), Animal Allies (*Tool 26, page 61*).

ENHANCING YOUR SPIRITUAL EQUILIBRIUM

Everything you do to keep yourself on an even keel, centred around an unshakeable sense of centredness in your spiritual *beingness*, is beneficial to all areas of your life, as is raising your vibrations and your consciousness to the highest possible levels.

One of the best ways of enhancing your spiritual equilibrium is through meditation. Meditation switches off the mind and places you in touch with a deeper reality. It's beneficial for your physical body and your spiritual health. And one of the easiest ways to quickly enter a meditative state is to gaze into the centre of a clear crystal.

CRYSTALS AND MEDITATION

Crystals have a natural affinity with meditation, as they calm your mind and open it to receive spiritual input. Your brain works in different frequencies, known as brainwaves, according to your state of consciousness, and holding a Smoky Quartz crystal, for instance, can help you to move between the beta brainwaves of everyday awareness and the alpha and theta brainwaves produced during meditation and altered states.

What you move into in meditation is a quiet state in which you don't try to do anything in particular. Some people like to focus on their breath or a candle flame, but simply being with a crystal removes the need to have a focus of this kind. It also facilitates allowing thoughts to move on through rather than trying to block them at source.

If you ever feel yourself 'going floaty' or drifting away during meditation (or at any other time), take your attention to the base of your spine and make a connection to the Earth or your crystal, or send down your grounding root (*see page 29*). Once you have your chakras under control (*see page 110*), opening the base chakra before meditation gives you an anchor and helps to ground your meditation into your body.

Treasure Chest

PHENACITE

Having an extremely high vibration, Phenacite connects your personal consciousness to a higher frequency, enabling you to contact the angelic realms, Ascended Masters and multi-dimensional levels of being. It brings refined spiritual frequencies to the Earth and integrates them. An excellent healer for the soul, it also downloads information from the Akashic Record to heal the source of dis-ease and the etheric blueprint.

Try This: Crystal Meditation

- Settle yourself in a quiet place, holding your crystal and making sure you won't be disturbed.
- Breathe gently and evenly, establishing a natural rhythm. As you breathe in, take in a sense of peace and let your body relax and soften. As you breathe out, let go of any tension or extraneous

thoughts or anxieties. Allow your body and your mind to settle into a quiet space.

- Take your attention to the base of your spine and feel its connection to the Earth.
- Hold the crystal in your hands, turn it until it catches the light and gaze into its mysterious depths. Breathe more deeply into your belly, consciously grounding spiritual energy and connecting more deeply with your crystal.
- Close your eyes. Let any thoughts or sounds drift past you and be aware only of the crystal in your hands, its energy and the spiritual clarity it brings to you. If you feel yourself drifting into thinking about everyday concerns, open your eyes and refocus on the crystal.
- After 10 to 20 minutes, bring your attention firmly back into the room and feel your feet firmly on the floor. Be aware of the grounding cord that goes from your feet deep down into the Earth to hold you gently in incarnation.

Crystal Tips for Meditation

- *Clear Quartz tunes out distractions. This stone naturally attunes itself to your vibration and takes your energy back to a state of spiritual perfection.*
- *The scintillating flashes of colour in Labradorite take you into another world, a heightened state of consciousness, and filter out any distractions.*
- *Bytownite and Spectrolite, higher-vibration forms of Labradorite, open the third eye and filter out distractions.*

- *Smoky Quartz enhances moving between alpha and beta brainwave states and calms the mind.*
- *Sodalite opens your higher awareness and stimulates spiritual perception, taking meditation to a deeper level.*
- *Higher-vibration crystals such as Azeztulite, Brandenberg and Vera Cruz Amethyst, Lemurian, Satyamani and Satyaloka Quartz, Petalite, Phenacite and Selenite, together with Blue Moonstone, Danburite or Nirvana Quartz (see The Crystal Bible, Volumes I, II and III, for details of these crystals), can take you further into expanded levels of consciousness and multi-dimensional worlds (see also Opening the Higher Chakras, page 223).*

Treasure Chest

FIRE AND ICE
Fire and Ice is a high vibration Quartz that has been thermally shocked. Its inner planes and rainbows take you travelling through multi-dimensions or deep into the Earth to make a powerful connection with the divine.

Crystals for Connecting with the Divine

Connection with divine energies and the spiritual level of being often occurs during meditation, when it's known as bliss consciousness or enlightenment, but you can be connected to divine energy all the time with the assistance of your crystal treasure chest. Connecting to this energy and anchoring it into a crystal means you'll always be connected to divine light at the heart of the universe and be part of the universal whole, the sea of spirit to which we all belong.

Try This: Anchoring Divine Light

Holding a crystal and gazing into its depths, be aware that the flashes of light you glimpse as you turn it are the light of the divine which is anchored to the crystal. Know that whenever you hold this crystal, you'll have an immediate connection to the divine.

Place the crystal to your forehead and absorb the divine light into your whole being.

Here's another exercise:

Try This: Travelling the Waves of Spirit

• Holding a Blue Lace Agate, Botswana Agate, Rainbow Obsidian or other banded stone or a Fire and Ice with its inner planes and inclusions, be aware of the gentle curves that flow over and beneath its surface. These are the waves in the sea of spirit to which we all belong.

- Trace these curves with your eye, letting them go a little out of focus.
- Travel the waves until you reach your spiritual home. Rest in this space and allow your soul to be refreshed.
- When you are ready to return, bring the stone to your soma chakra at the hairline and anchor the connection there.
- Make sure you ground yourself thoroughly via your grounding cord as you stand up.

Attuning to Unconditional Love

If you always feel bathed in unconditional love, you'll never need to know fear or dread. Rose Quartz is an excellent stone for attuning to unconditional love, but all the pink stones and many of the white ones, such as Selenite, are crystallized love, so use whichever stone you feel attracted to.

Try This: Experiencing Unconditional Love

Holding a Rose Quartz or Mangano Calcite, allow yourself to feel the unconditional love radiating out from its serene core. This is the love at the heart of the universe which emanates through all things. Place the stone over your heart and allow your heart to absorb this unconditional divine love. Feel it flood through your whole being.

OPENING THE HIGHER CHAKRAS

As already mentioned, in addition to the traditional seven chakras, several more chakras are opening in response to universal energy changes at this time, and your spiritual equilibrium is facilitated by having these chakras open and functioning under your control as they filter and anchor multi-dimensional realities into the earth plane. These 'higher' chakras vibrate at a different, faster rate and are more able to channel refined spiritual energies down through you and up from the Earth. Through this change in the core vibration of your energy bodies, 'lower' frequency energies simply cannot reach you.

Several 'new' crystals have become available to activate these higher chakras, some of which are expensive and difficult to source. Tugtupite, for instance, is rare, as it's only found in Greenland, but you can use Danburite, which is in itself a high-vibration stone (though not quite as rarified as Tugtupite), or one of the pink Azeztulites, to open the heart seed chakra if Tugtupite is not available. Satyamani and Satyaloka Quartz are specially infused with high spiritual energies by Indian mountain monks, and these work well with Nirvana Quartz from the high Himalayas to open the higher crown chakras. If you cannot obtain the exact crystals you need, when programming the crystals that are available ask that the energy is lifted up to its highest level in order to receive the influx of new vibrations. Green Ridge Quartz is excellent for this.

However, these new chakras can only be opened when you're properly attuned and ready for the influx of energy that accompanies the opening, so don't try to hurry the process. Open one or two at first and then allow the energy to be assimilated. Then open another and so on until all the higher chakras have been opened.

THE HIGHER CHAKRAS

- *Higher earth:* Paradoxically the 'higher' earth chakra is below the earth chakra, about a foot below your feet. This chakra links to the Earth's subtle etheric bodies and the subtle energy grid surrounding the planet. It mediates the inflow of rarified earth energy that helps you to stabilize and assimilate refined spiritual energies reaching the Earth whilst remaining grounded in your physical body.

- *Heart seed:* Just beneath the breastbone, this chakra helps you to remember the reason why you're in incarnation and connects you to the divine plan for your soul evolution. It is a chakra of infinite compassion.

- *Higher heart:* A place of unconditional love and compassion, this chakra helps you to radiate forgiveness and acceptance out to the planet and to yourself.

- *Soma:* With this chakra open you're in a place of total spiritual connection and higher consciousness aligned with the purpose for which you're on Earth.

- *Soul star:* With this chakra activated, you can channel the highest self-illumination and spiritual light into your physical body, which will raise its vibrations accordingly.

- *Stellar gateway:* This cosmic doorway leads to other dimensions and connects you to the highest energies in the cosmos, enabling you to communicate with enlightened beings.

Activating your Higher Chakras

It's wise to take this activation slowly, working on one or two chakras at a time and gradually building up to opening them all and allowing the influx of energy that follows.

A sensible order would be to open the higher earth chakra and the heart seed and link the heart seed to the higher heart. Then, after you have opened the soma chakra and assimilated the energy, move on to the higher crown chakras one at a time, always asking that the crystals filter and mediate the energy so that you can receive it at the optimum strength for your personal vibration. The influx of energy can be slowly increased as you become more attuned to the multi-dimensional levels you are contacting. Remember that you can always activate one or two of the chakras, take a break for as long as you need and then resume the process.

The Activation Process

- Hold all the crystals you are using for the exercise for a few moments, visualizing them bathed in bright white light.

- Lie down and position the crystals as appropriate according to the chakra(s) you're activating today. Build slowly on the previous work you've done by laying stones on all the chakras already activated (*see page 110*) and the new chakras as follows:

  * Smoky and Elestial Quartz about a foot below your feet.

  * Tugtupite or Danburite on the heart seed at the base of the breastbone.

* Rose Quartz or Mangano Calcite three fingers' width above the heart.

* Preseli Bluestone or Ammolite on your hairline (soma chakra).

* White Elestial Quartz or Nirvana Quartz on your crown.

* Phenacite, Petalite or Satyamani Quartz about a foot above your crown (point-down if your crystal has a point).

* Brandenberg or Satyaloka Quartz above the soul star.

• Take your attention down to the crystal below your feet and be aware of the higher earth chakra opening. Feel how it pulls in refined earth energies and radiates them up to the Smoky Quartz and through your whole body. Be aware of your connection to the Earth's energy meridians and feel how the Elestial lifts them to a higher vibration. Feel yourself aligning to the faster, and purer, vibration it carries.

• Now take your attention up to the heart seed chakra. When this chakra opens you are flooded with infinite compassion and divine connection.

• Take your attention to the higher heart chakra. Feel it open and expand, receiving and radiating unconditional love and awakening your innate compassion and connection with others. Feel how this chakra connects to the throat chakra so you can communicate love out to the world.

• When you reach the soma chakra, feel how much more of your own higher energy can make contact with the part of you that is in incarnation and become aware of your soul plan for the present lifetime.

- Take your attention up to the chakras above your head. Be aware of your connection to higher spiritual guidance and other dimensions. Feel how the energy flows down into the crystals, activating esoteric awareness and soul memory. Know you are a spiritual being on a human journey and you have the support of many higher beings on that journey. Allow as much of the high-dimensional universal energy to flow down through your body as you can easily assimilate.

- When the activation is complete, slowly remove the crystals, starting with the highest crown chakra and working down to the higher earth chakra.

- When you reach the higher earth chakra, be aware there is a grounding cord which links your feet to this chakra. This cord keeps you grounded within your physical body and connected to the Earth.

- Finally, pick up the crystal from the higher earth chakra. Stand up and feel your feet firmly on the ground.

- Repeat the exercise daily until the activation is complete.

Crystal Tip for Higher Chakra Activation

Laying the various colours of Green Ridge Quartz from your solar plexus right up to your throat, third eye, crown and higher crown (above your head) rapidly activates and harmonizes all the higher chakras.

FEELING POSITIVE

By now you will be able to turn a negative emotion or thought about yourself into a positive one and re-vision the past and will have freed yourself from any self-fulfilling cycle of negative expectation. Feeling positive about yourself, identifying your resources, boosting your self-esteem and your self-respect are the greatest gifts you can give yourself. Believe you are worth something and you are. If you don't feel demeaned by anything you do, for instance, no matter what your job, you're able to do it with good grace and enjoyment of the contribution you make to society, and for the sheer pleasure of doing something well, rather than for the financial reward. This brings about a deep inner peace and radiates goodwill that enhances the environment all around you.

Treasure Chest

ECLIPSE STONE

Eclipse stone stimulates both inner sight and insight, taking you deep into yourself to explore the sacred, set-aside and taboo areas of life.
It is a great support during times of change. Enhancing clarity of thought, it helps you to plan ahead and yet be flexible enough to go with the unfolding flow if circumstances show that the plan is inappropriate for your soul growth. It rolls away whatever is hiding the truth, releasing emotional blockages, memories and ancestral patterns, and brings the shadow into the light.

Try This: Identifying your Gifts and Abilities

You will need your journal and a pen.

- Take your phone off the hook and put a 'Do not disturb' notice on your door.
- If you find music soothing, play suitable background music or you can choose silence.
- Sit quietly and focus your thoughts inwards. Let the distractions of the outer world slip away. Remind yourself that your intent is to identify and clarify all your gifts, skills and abilities, the resources you know about, those you haven't yet recognized and those as yet unmanifest.
- Breathe gently, focusing on your breath. As you breathe out, allow any tension you may be feeling to drop away. As you breathe in, feel yourself filling up with a sense of peace and relaxation.
- When you feel ready, pick up your journal and pen and make a heading:

'My Gifts'

- Ask yourself, 'What is my greatest gift?' Keep asking that question and write down the answers that come into your mind. Don't censor them. Be open to all possibilities and paradoxes, no matter how small, silly or irrelevant they may seem. Remind yourself that they are precious gifts, a part of your soul learning.
- When you've finished the list, read it through and give yourself a pat on the back. Congratulate yourself on having such skills and abilities. Don't

stint on the praise for yourself – appreciate yourself and show gratitude for those gifts, whether they are natural talents or hard-won skills. Be appreciative, recognize your Self in these qualities and abilities, honour yourself and have confidence.

- Place the notebook under your pillow and tell yourself that during the night any further insights you need will rise up into your consciousness so you can add them to the list when you wake. Pay particular attention to any dreams you may have. Whenever you recall or recognize another gift, add it to the list.

CREATING YOUR LIFE PLAN

As a karmic astrologer, I believe we all incarnate with a life plan and a knowledge of our soul's purpose. This is shown in our birth chart. So, for me, reading a chart reveals a life plan. But you don't need to have your chart read, you can access your life plan now.

Fortunately your higher self (the spiritual part of you that is only partially in incarnation and which knows far more than the-you-down-here does and which has an overview of the full breadth of your soul experience) keeps a record of your purpose and tracks how well you are doing with manifesting the life plan that you set in place before you incarnated. Meeting your higher self allows you to access the plan and to gain valuable assistance with manifesting it more fully in your life now. A Phantom Quartz crystal assists this journey, as it facilitates negotiating higher levels of being, but a Cathedral Quartz, which connects directly to the Akashic Record that holds information of all that has been or will be is also helpful, as is a Brandenberg Amethyst or one of the higher chakra crystals on pages 225–226.

Before starting this journey, turn your phone off and ensure that you will not be disturbed.

Accessing your Life Plan

- Cleanse and dedicate your crystal to obtaining information on your life plan. Hold it in whichever hand feels more comfortable or place it over the soma chakra at the middle of your hairline above your third eye.

- Sit or lie comfortably and breathe gently and easily, bringing your attention into yourself.
If you have any thoughts that do not belong to the journey you are making, simply let them pass on by without giving them attention.

- Continue to breathe gently, establishing a slow, deep rhythm and feeling your connection with the crystal in your hand. Picture yourself standing in front of a lift (if you don't like enclosed spaces you can use a long escalator that climbs high into the sky above your head). As the doors open (or you step onto the escalator), step in and ask your crystal to take you to meet your higher self. You will see that there is a button marked 'higher self'. Press this and feel the lift moving rapidly upwards (or let the escalator take you up).

- When the lift stops, step out and ask your higher self to be there to meet you or ask to be directed to where your higher self is waiting.

- Spend as long as you need to with your higher self, reviewing the life plan you made before incarnation and the reasons for this. Check out with your higher self whether this plan is still appropriate for you and if not, make any necessary amendments.

- If it is not clear how you can activate your life plan or if you are way off track, ask your higher self for guidance and, if necessary, ask to be taken to the planning meeting at which you, your guides and helpers planned your present incarnation. Use the crystal in your hand as an anchor and *aide-mémoire* so that you will remember.

- When you are ready to return, thank your higher self for the assistance you have received and make your way to the lift (or escalator). If possible, ask your higher self to enter the lift with you to come down to your starting point with you so that this higher wisdom will be easily available to you.

- If appropriate, make an appointment with your higher self for a regular meeting at which your progress can be assessed and further assistance gained.

- When you step out at the bottom of the lift (or off the escalator), bring the memory and the insights with you. Bring your attention fully back into the room, stand up and move around, stamping your feet to reconnect to the Earth.

- As soon as possible, write up the experience in your journal, holding your crystal and noting down your life plan and any amendments that were necessary or advice that you received.

If your life plan was not immediately accessible to you, trust that you will become aware of it in as appropriate a way as possible and with the right timing for your soul development; watch out for signs and signals from the universe as to what this might be.

Now all you have to do is trust that your timeline will unfold in accordance with your soul's life plan and your own highest good.

SETTING GOALS

A great many of the stresses and strains of modern living arise out of having expectations instead of goals and visions. One of the easiest ways to ensure your life flows smoothly is to make a timeline that has goals and gifts along the way but is flexible enough to cope with change.

Begin by writing down a list of all you wish for in your journal – and check out which are expectations of how things should be and which are hopes for what might be.

Then set yourself some realistic goals. Being happy and feeling abundant without necessarily having huge wealth, for example, would be a more productive goal than winning the lottery.

Treasure Chest

SCAPOLITE

Scapolite is an excellent stone for helping you to set goals and make changes. Useful if you need to look deep inside yourself to find the source of problems, it helps you to overcome self-sabotage and become independent-minded. It can be programmed to help you fulfil your life plan.

Try This: Visioning the Crystal Timeline

- When you've identified all the goals you'd like to put in place, think about the skills you'll need or the gifts that will enable them to come to fruition more easily. Close your eyes and picture a timeline going back from where you stand now and forward into the future.
- At many points along the 'past line' you'll see crystals sparkling. Go back and pick them up. These are gifts and skills you can take forward into the future.
- Walk forward along the timeline, seeding it with crystals as you go to represent the gifts you have and the goals to which you are attaching them. Recognize that this timeline is flexible – it can adapt to cope with change – but the gifts will be there whenever you need them.
- Come back into the present moment, knowing that when the time is right you will be able to utilize the gifts to manifest your goals and fulfil your life plan.

Treasure Chest

GREEN RIDGE IRON-COATED QUARTZ

This crystal reaches all the areas that couldn't normally be released. The dark iron entraps material not needed in the energetic body. As the coating flakes away so the negativity is removed.

ORANGE GREEN RIDGE QUARTZ

Highly energizing and creative, this crystal cleanses the sacral chakra of previous relationship hooks and stimulates standing in your own power.

GREEN RIDGE LIGHT-GOLDEN PLATE QUARTZ

This crystal acts as a life support system while healing work is being done. It is particularly helpful for activating and purifying the chakras in the upper body.

CLEAR GREEN RIDGE QUARTZ

Excellent for drawing in healing and transmutational energy, this crystal brings enlightenment, light into every cell of your being and opens the higher crown chakras.

AMETHYST GREEN RIDGE QUARTZ

This crystal has an incredibly high spiritual vibration that connects to the highest dimensions and to unity consciousness. Opening the highest of the chakras, it brings in a whole new meaning to spiritual connection.

FINDING ABUNDANCE

For many people security is a matter of money, but true abundance is a state of mind, not money in the bank or material possessions. When you enjoy abundance you feel fulfilled and rich on every level of your being and therefore protected.

There is a story about a man who, before he went to India, was told by his spiritual teacher that he would meet a great teacher there who would give him the most important gift that was to be gained in life.

The man travelled around India from ashram to ashram and sat at the feet of many gurus, but felt he had learned little and received no gift. On his last night he went for a walk along the beach and saw an old man sitting in the sand, all alone. As he had a few rupees left, he went over to give them to the man, whom he assumed to be a beggar. He was surprised to find his offering refused with a smile.

'I have everything I need right here,' said the old man, pointing to the sand and the sea, which were bathed in the red glow of sunset, 'but bless you for offering. It's all here, share it with me for a while.'

They sat quietly together in companionable silence, watching the sun slide into the sea.

When the man returned home his teacher asked if he'd found his gift. 'No,' he replied. 'I sat at the feet of many gurus but there was nothing.'

'Are you sure?' asked his teacher. 'Tell me, who impressed you most?'

'None of the gurus,' he replied, 'only an old man on a beach who refused the money I offered because he had everything he needed right there.'

After a few moments of silence he suddenly said: 'Oh yes, I see now, that is the greatest gift. That man was perfectly happy and yet he had nothing.'

The man had gained the gift of an abundant heart.

Treasure Chest

GROSSULAR GARNET

Garnet has long been used for its protective and life-enhancing energies and Grossular Garnet is particularly effective, especially in its raw state, for creating a crystal grid which has a naturally sacred shape and which draws in abundance and helps it to manifest in your life. Particularly helpful in lawsuits, Grossular Garnet helps you to find ingenious solutions through cooperative effort. It also overcomes mistrust and stress-related disease.

GOLDSTONE

Goldstone is a product of alchemy, a glass infused with copper to create shining points of light. It is a powerful attractor and manifestation tool. It is a stone of drive and ambition, boosting your motivation and the courage to manifest what you most desire. The stone helps you to discover your inner wealth and gives you the patience to wait until the timing is exactly right before revealing it.

THE ABUNDANCE CEREMONY

You will need:
- a journal and pen
- a golden cloth
- 6 Grossular Garnets or other abundance stones (*see page 241*)
- a gold candle in a suitable holder
- matches.

Preparation
- Take your phone off the hook and put a 'Do not disturb' notice on your door.
- If you find music soothing, play suitable background music, or you can choose to prepare in silence.
- Sit quietly and focus your thoughts inward. Let the distractions of the outer world slip away.
- Remind yourself that your intent is to connect to abundance and that this ceremony is to bring abundance more fully into manifestation in your life.
- Breathe gently, focusing on your breath. As you breathe out, allow any tension you may be feeling to drop away. As you breathe in, feel yourself filling up with a sense of peace and relaxation.
- When you feel ready, ask yourself what your present definition of abundance is and how you would like it to manifest in your life. Be specific and precise, but don't censor what comes into your mind. Be open to all possibilities and paradoxes. Think sideways and

out of the box and allow yourself to consider areas of abundance you haven't approached before.

• Leaving the first page blank, write each point down in your journal. Give it plenty of space. Let it breathe.

• Now think of all the ways in which abundance already manifests in your life: friends, talents, qualities, whatever comes to mind...

• Place your journal under your pillow and tell yourself that during the night any further insights you need will rise up into your consciousness so you can note them down when you wake. Pay particular attention to any dreams you may have.

A continuous hexagram

The Ceremony

• Have a bath or shower and put on clean clothes.

• Dim the lights and, if you wish, play suitable background music. Alternatively, you can work the ceremony in silence.

• Now take your journal and read through it. Distil the essence of what you consider abundance into one sentence and write it on the page you left blank, starting with 'Abundance is…' (You may also like to make a note of it on a piece of paper so you can read it aloud as part of the ceremony.)

• Spread the cloth onto a table and slowly and deliberately place the six abundance stones in a continuous hexagram pattern to create abundance on all levels and in all dimensions (*see illustration on page 239*). As you place the stones, say, 'I am placing these stones to manifest abundance more fully in my life at every level of my being.'

• Place your journal in the centre with the candle above it. Light the candle and look deep into the flame.

• Affirm to yourself that the abundance is already there for you, waiting to come into manifestation right now.

• Call your abundance into being. Read out the sentence that sums up the essence of your abundance and say: 'I call it into being now.'

• Put your hand on your heart and sit quietly, feeling abundance flowing through you. Feel the satisfaction and excitement it gives you. See yourself enjoying this abundance as the future stretches out before you and pull that future into the ever-present now.

• When you're ready, blow the candle out, sending your abundance out into the world with the smoke. Thank the universe for granting your request. Be confident it is returning to you in tangible form.

• Leave your abundance statement with the layout for several days. Each morning light the candle and call your abundance into being, feeling delighted anticipation as you do so. Thank the universe for listening. Blow out the candle and trust that abundance is manifesting in the best way possible for you. You need do nothing more than allow it to happen.

Crystal Tips for Abundance
Ammolite, Aventurine, Candle Quartz, Carnelian, Chalcopyrite, Chrysoprase, Cinnabar, Citrine, Diamond, Emerald, Goldstone, Green Calcite, Green Moss Agate, Grossular Garnet, Jade, Malachite, Manifestation Quartz, Peridot, Iron Pyrite, Ruby, Sapphire, Tiger's Eye, Topaz.

Manifestation Quartz
Manifestation stones help to bring about abundance but work at many levels to manifest what you need, including bringing your dreams into being. If you need to manifest *more* of anything, a manifestation crystal assists you. This interesting formation has one or more small crystals totally enclosed within a larger one. Such a crystal often lies unrecognized among Quartz crystals, waiting for your eye to alight on it. When it does, take it home, programme it carefully, stand it on a window ledge in sunlight or in the far left-hand corner of your home (the wealth corner in

Feng Shui practice) and allow it to do its work. It functions best when programmed for the good of everyone.

Crystal Tips for Manifestation

Ammolite, Apatite, Black Actinolite (manifests new energies), Blue Aragonite (manifests your soul plan), Blue Moonstone (manifests higher-dimensional space), Grossular Garnet, Kyanite (manifests spiritual connection), Manifestation Quartz, Okenite (manifests your highest Self), Red Chalcedony (manifests your dreams), Stillbite (manifests action), Tiger's Eye (manifests your will), Topaz (manifests your goals), Zincite.

FEEDING YOUR BODY AND SOUL

One of the most powerful ways to feel safe is to feed your soul. If you look on beauty, walk in nature, watch the clouds go by, cultivate joy and are kind to yourself, doing the things that give you pleasure, you'll naturally feel bright inside and that light will protect you. If you're fortunate enough to have the seasons to follow, you can chart the growth of snowdrops and primroses in the spring and the turn of the leaves in the autumn and watch out for the first snowflake. If you live by the sea, you can swim with dolphins, or on land you can be with dogs or horses. Simply looking at a beautiful view feeds your soul, but walking the hills or the forests takes you right in among God's creation. And if you energize your food with crystals your body, too, can be fed with spiritual nourishment.

Try This: Energize your Food

- Lay out four Quartz crystals with their points facing inwards around your plate before you eat, asking that the crystal energy infuse the food.
- Alternatively, use bright red or orange crystals or eat off a crystal plate (remember to cleanse it energetically first).

COUNTING YOUR BLESSINGS

Counting your blessings has long been recognized as a way to increase them and to feed your soul. I have a friend who constantly says, 'I am blessed,' and everything in the world falls into place for her. She has a beautiful home with a stunning view of the sea, exactly what she envisioned before moving on at a time when her life was at a low ebb, and she is thankful for her life every day. If she needs a place to stay while away, someone offers her their home; when she travels planes are never late and obstacles simply melt away under her positive focus. She feels truly blessed and affirms that every day.

Focusing on the positive, the things that work and the things that give you joy, and giving thanks for them, reinforces all you're doing to feel safe and cope with change. Recording and rereading your successes is an excellent way to strengthen the cycle. You can either enter your blessings in your general journal or create a special blessings journal you write in each day. Choosing a special coloured pen with which you write only your blessings makes them extra special.

If you're using a special blessings journal, make a title page: 'My Blessings'.

If you're using your general journal, make a special entry each day under 'Daily Blessing'. Whenever you feel down, read your journal and remember how blessed you are.

The blessings journal helps you to identify the gift in any situation, no matter how bleak it may seem at the time. A relationship may have ended, for example, and then you may have found you actually liked living in solitude and taking the time to get to know and like yourself – this is a potent blessing. Peridot is an extremely useful stone for helping you to see the blessing in all things.

The ideal time to start counting your blessings is at the dark of the moon, just before the new moon makes itself known in the sky.

Try This

- Write a list of all the things you feel thankful for or blessed by. Begin each sentence: 'I feel thankful for...', 'I am happy that...', 'I am grateful for...' or 'I am blessed by...', as this strengthens your positive emotions and feeling of being blessed each time you write.

- When you've run out of blessings, say thank you for all those blessings and feel the gratitude in your heart radiating out to bless all those with whom you came into contact.

- Now think about the negative situations in your life and focus on what you learned from them (hold a Peridot if you feel at all wary of or puzzled by this exercise). Write the gifts in your journal and say thank you for all those blessings and feel the gratitude in your heart radiating out to bless all those with whom you came into contact.

- Each night take a few moments to count the blessings of the day and to record them in your journal.

You can keep a large Spirit Quartz on or alongside your journal to multiply the blessings and radiate them out into your environment.

Crystal Tips for Blessings

Amethyst, Clear or Citrine Spirit Quartz, Elestial Quartz, Green Ridge Quartz, Larimar, Lavender Quartz, Mangano Calcite, Morganite, Muscovite, Peridot, Rose Quartz, Strombolite.

HOLDING THE VISION

During the period I was re-visioning this book I was, ironically, visually impaired. A series of operations had left my eyes in a poor state and I was only slowly regaining my capacity to see – both outwardly and inwardly. The experience had left me in a bad place, unable to use my psychic abilities, to meditate or to reach out to others. But, even in the most desperate of days, there was always a bright star leading me onwards.

Sitting in the pit

I'd had a cataract operation and had barely left the house for almost five months. Simple, you might think. But no. Mine was a 'complex' case, to quote the surgeon, and it triggered the cataract in the other eye to grow overnight. I was virtually blind and utterly disorientated for three months before the other eye was operated on. Equally complex. So, two more months passed before I could see again. It gave me a lot of time to ponder the deeper questions of life, like 'Why?' Normally, or so well-meaning people told me, if your outer sight shuts down your inner sight opens up. Err, no. I thought, *I have to see things in a different light.*

I've been in dark places before but had never been quite that restricted. I was so disorientated and sun-blind that I couldn't relate to the outside world at all. I took one day at a time, and did much inward thinking. But I came to realize that I was being asked to relate to tiny details that I probably wouldn't have noticed before, and it became a place of deep transformation.

Initially I sat clutching my guidestone, intoning to myself 'This too will pass.' Then I realized that it wouldn't until I accepted the situation I was in, so I immersed myself and got on with simply being here no matter what. I had to love the state I was in. Mindfulness and the power of now had to be explored at a very deep level, and I needed to acknowledge and accept how I was feeling moment to moment, and then let it go. Thank goodness for astrology, because this, as always, helped me to understand what was going on and where I was sitting in the greater scheme of things. If you find yourself in a similar place, I would urge you to have an astrological reading to shine a light into the darkness.

Pink stars

One very bright light shone into the darkness of what I came to call my 'pit'. My granddaughter (who lives quite a distance away) was pregnant, and throughout the gestation I talked to the new soul who was incarnating. I could feel this little being waving to me across the ether. I missed her birth as I was still recovering, but we've met since, old friends reunited.

My great-granddaughter, Charlie-Skye, is a pink star child. Highly alert from the first, fully present with wise, all-knowing eyes that look deep into your soul (well, she is a Scorpio after all), and exuding such tender love. Pink stars are linked to Archangel Chamuel, the archangel who inspires us to realize that in order to love others we must first love ourselves.

Charlie-Skye's hands are very active. One of the first pictures of her shows her making a peace sign. From her birthchart she's clearly been here before, and she's already started to live out her healing purpose. A number of these children have been born lately, and it's going to be fascinating to watch their soul plans unfold and the impact they have on our world.

I am very thankful that I have the eyes to see these little miracles. I treasure my sight, inner and outer, in a way that was not available to me before. Funnily enough, in July I am leading an astrological retreat to explore the gifts of Pluto, the planet of alchemical transformation. I'll be lighting my miner's lamp, grasping my guidestone and setting off into the Underworld with confidence. I know the way intimately by now. And, of course, I can feel my way through the dark knowing that I am fully protected!

BEING IN THE PRESENT MOMENT

Since most things you worry about are in the future and positive experiences such as joy and serenity are in the present moment, staying in that present moment means you can put aside your worries and allow yourself to relax without having to do or even be anything. I think this is best expressed by Margaret Koolman:

Let there be nothing to be 'gained' by doing what just came to your mind, just do it with all attention and focus.

Make what you are doing the most interesting thing, so that the tendrils of your thinking don't distract you.

Make it the most sensuous thing, feeling with your fingertips and eyes, so that your body won't distract you.

Put your heart into it, so that your emotions won't distract you from this moment, this activity, this precious decision you have made.

For in this commitment you will meet your soul, and the activity will be done together, in sweet harmony and love.

Margaret Koolman[11]

One of the most potent ways of creating this 'sweet harmony and love' is sitting with one of the deeply spiritual crystals and doing nothing other than quietly contemplating it until you become one with it in its slow and easy rhythm of life that only takes a breath every hundred years or so.

Try This: Being with a Crystal

- Hold whichever of your crystals feels to you as though it holds the most light, most love and most serenity at this moment in time.
- Contemplate your crystal quietly. Be aware of its shape, its colour and how it fits into your hand. If it is transparent, gaze into it. If it is opaque, gently trace the colours and patterns on its surface.
- Allow yourself to blend with the stone, to take a long slow breath that lasts for a hundred years so it is always the perpetual now, there is no moving on to something, no coming from somewhere, only the eternal present moment that has been and is forever.
- When the time comes to turn your attention back to the world, bring that eternal present moment with you and tuck it inside your heart and mind. Simply be.

Afterword

Once you've energetically strengthened your boundaries, developed a positive mindset and ensured you remain grounded with your subtle energies high, there is one more thing to remember: pay attention to your language and your intentions. It's easy to slip back into negativity, to create that gap into which something can slide, simply by the unwise use of language, as the words you choose affect how you approach something. So, when change comes into your life, call it a challenge not a crisis, a decluttering not a loss, an opportunity not a redundancy. Never say 'That always happens to me' when faced with a repeating pattern, nor 'I'll never be able to do that' when faced with a challenge. By now you have learned how to turn thoughts around, so positively affirm your intention and set a goal and you will be well on the way to manifesting your vision.

Remember the three golden rules for psychic safety:

1. Don't meddle with things you don't understand.
2. Stay focused and positive and keep things in proportion.
3. Retain a sense of humour at all times.

And finally, stop worrying and start living joyously.

After that, all that remains is to believe and be.

Notes and References

If you are in any doubt as to whether a crystal may be toxic or not, please consult the list on my website (www. judyhall.co.uk) which is updated regularly.

1. Dion Fortune, *Psychic Self-Defence*, Rider, 1931; quotation from *Psychic Self-Defense*, Samuel Weiser, Maine, 2001, p.227
2. See my books *The Book of Why* and *The Soulmate Myth*, both Flying Horse Press, 2010
3. See my book *Psychic Development* (Flying Horse Press, 2014) for details of how a group of scientists deliberately created a psychic communicator who took on a life of his own.
4. For an extremely comprehensive and useful list of animal allies and their attributes, see http://www. animalspirits.com/index1.html and Celia Gunn's *Simply Totem Animals* (Zambezi, 2011).
5. For EFT training in the USA and for a free manual and newsletter, see garycraig@emofree.com
6. The most powerful means of protection against computer emanations I have found is the Computer Clear program from World Development Systems (*see Resources*). It runs continuously on your computer

and feeds healing energies to you to counteract electromagnetic stress.

7. For further measures, see my book *Good Vibrations: Psychic protection, energy enhancement and space clearing* (Flying Horse Press, 2008), also Wilma Davidson's *Spirit Rescue* (Llewellyn, 2007).

8. See *Good Vibrations*. Many thanks to Margaret Cahill for allowing me to use pretty much verbatim the information on Crystal EFT from that book.

9. See *Good Vibrations* for details on lifting the curse imposed by the juju man.

10. There's an enormous body of research now available on how altering your stance alters your brain chemistry.

11. Margaret Koolman, 'New Moon in Pisces', *Soul Astrology* newsletter, 25 February 1995, www.soulastrology.com

Resources

Crystal Suppliers
- Crystals specially attuned for you by Judy Hall are available from www.angeladditions.co.uk
- www.exquisitecrystals.com
- www.hehishelo.co.uk
- EvoLuZion, www.adrianmieras.com and www.crystalhealingcourses.com, supply excellent-quality Tugtupite jewellery and stones.

Flower and Crystal Essence Suppliers
- Petaltone Essences: www.Petaltone.co.uk
- Living Tree Orchid Essences and the International Flower Essence Repertoire, Achamore House, Isle of Gigha, Argyll, Scotland, PA41 7AD; gigha@atlas.co.uk
- Alaskan Essences: www.Alaskanessences.com
- Bush Essences: www.ausflowers.com.au
- Indigo Essences: www.Indigoessences.com
- Bailey Essences: www.essencesonline.com
- Green Man Tree Essences: www.greenmantrees.demon.co.uk
- Crystal Balance Company has a range of protective, cleansing, and soul- and confidence-building essences: www.crystalbalance.co.uk

Chakra Creams
- NHR Organic Oils: www.organicaromatherapy.co.uk

Supplier of Computer Clear Program

World Development Systems Ltd: www.wds-global.com and www.computerclear.com; e-mail: info@wds-global.com

Note: Although Computer Clear is not yet available for Macs, running Silent Healing, also available from World Development Systems Ltd, has the same protective effect.

Psychic Training

The College of Psychic Studies
16 Queensberry Place
London SW7 2ER
www.collegeofpsychicstudies.co.uk

Spirit Release Practitioners

• The Spirit Release Foundation: www.spiritrelease.com
• School of Intuition and Healing:
   www intuitionandhealing.co.uk/

EFT

• EFT USA: free manual and newsletter: garycraig@emofree.com

Workshops and Karmic Readings

www.judyhall.co.uk (Judy is not able to enter into correspondence or work on psychic protection or spirit release).

Further Reading

- Allen, Sue, *Spirit Release: A practical handbook*, O Books, 2007
- Davidson, Wilma, *Spirit Rescue*, Llewellyn, Min., 2007
- Hall, Judy, *The Crystal Bible*, Volumes I, II and III, Godsfield Press, 2003 and 2009
- —, *Crystal Healing*, Godsfield Press, 2005
- —, *Crystal Prescriptions*, O Books, 2006
- —, *Crystal Love*, Godsfield Press, 2007
- —, *Psychic Development*, Flying Horse Press, 2014
- —, *The Crystal Experience*, Godsfield Press, 2010
- —, *Crystals and Sacred Sites*, Fair Winds Press, 2012
- —, *Earth Blessings*, Watkins, 2014
- —, *The Book of Why*, Flying Horse Press, 2010
- —, *The Soulmate Myth*, Flying Horse Press, 2010
- —, *The Life-Changing Crystals*, Godsfield Press, 2012
- —, *The Crystal Wisdom Oracle*, Watkins Books, 2014
- —, *101 Power Crystals,* Fair Winds Press, 2012
- Schwartz, Rob, *Courageous Souls*, Whispering Winds Press, 2006
- www.watkinsreview.com
- White, Ian, *Bush Flower Healing*, Bantam, 1999

Index

Note: coloured or different varieties of a crystal appear within the main entry for the type of crystal. Treasure Chest entries are in **bold**.

A

Abandonment 14, 148
Abundance 148, 236–42
Actinolite 49, 59, 242
Addictions 170
Adrenaline 112, 142
Aegirine 44, 49, 126
Affirmations 7, 20, 36, 116, 143, 147, 156, 165, 166, 188, 193, 196, 216
Agate 4, 59, 171, 173
    Banded 55
    Blue Lace 17, 18, 93, 111, 150, 152, 156, 221
    Botswana 221
    Dendritic 92
    Fire 30, 156
    Moss **58**, 59, 156, 241
    Snakeskin 65, 153, 166
    Tree 59, 65, 92
Age of Aquarius xii
Ajoite 46, 101, 213
Akashic Record 216, 218, 231
Altar 42, 95–6
Amazonite 8, 71, 73, **74**, 88, 156, 166
Amber 8, 10, 20, 30, 36, 49, 98, 101, 102, 173, **206**, 207, 208
Amethyst 8, 17, 20, **22**, 65, 66, 92, 101, 111, 116, 126, 127, 144, 150, 151, 152, 156, 170, 171, 172, 174, 186, 210, 246

Brandenberg 6, 9, **21**, 33, 65, 91, 126, 153, 171, 231, 226
    Smoky 126
    Vera Cruz 220
Ametrine 124
Ammolite 44, **211**, 242
Amphibole *see* Quartz
Amulets 4, l5, 16, 37, 184
Angelite 46
Angels 8, 16, 35, 41, 44–6, 49, 53, 56, 102, 125, 156, 161, 171, 184, 189, 190, 195, 200
Angel's Hair *see* Rutilated Quartz
Angelsword 126
Anger 14, 71, 72, 88, 112, 113, 121, 131, 135, 147, 148, 157, 169, 171, 179, 185, 192, 200
    release 135, 152
Animal allies 53, 61, 64, 200, 216
    crystals connections to 64
Apache Tear 10, 49, 101, 102
Apatite 242
Apophyllite 38, **39**, 115, 171
Aquamarine 10, 46, 49
Aragonite, all colours 30, 87, 92, 242
Archangel Michael 47, 82
Artemesia 55, 79
Astral Clear 76–7, 81, 82, 83, 124–6

Atlantasite 87, 92
Aura x, xxiv, 8, 11, 25, 48, 81, 85,
        97, 98, 99, 100, 101, 102,
        105, 121, 123, 129, 149, 150,
        169, 191
    Repairing 100
Auralite 23 55
Aventurine, Green 8, 18, 92, 111,
        116, 117, 118, 121, **122**, 124,
        125, 142, 150, 152, 196, 241
Azeztulite 220, 223
Azurite with Malachite 38

B

Belief xvi, xxvi, 13, 32, 58, 59,
        134, 156, 162, 164, 167, 183,
        185, 187, 188
Belly breathing 27
Beryl 171, 173
Blessings 56, 57, 95, 198, 208,
        245
Bloodstone xxi, 92, 101, 114, 116
        127, 129, 144, 151, 171
Blue Euclase **57**, 59, 61
Boab 126
Body language xx, 213–16
Boji Stones 28, 30
Boundaries xix, xxx, xxxii, 3, 61,
        63, 73, 75, 97, 103, 124, 156,
        166, 183, 190, 251
Brainwaves 217
Brandenberg see Amethyst
Brazilianite **103**
Bronzite 10, 30, 49, 192
Brown crystals 28
Brown rice 12
Bubble of light xxv, 20, 22, 46,
        98, 120, 121, 124, 160, 161,
        178, 193, 200, 206
Bumble Bee Jasper **63**, 64
Bytownite (Yellow Labradorite) 38,
        39, 121, 219

C

Calcite
    Angel's Wing 19, 45, 46
    Black see Master Shamanite
    Green 172, 241
    Honey 171
    Mangano 57, 152, 156, 171,
        177, 222, 225, 245
    Orange 7
    Red 14, 78
Carnelian xxi, 12, 14, 16, 44, 78,
        93, 129, **145**, 146, 152, 156,
        171, 241
    Orange 93, 111, 150, 175
Celestite 8, **45**, 46, 210
Celestobarite 55, 64
Cellular memory 54
Ceremony xxxii, 40–2, 157–8, 166,
        238, 240
Chalcedony 36
    Blue 92, 196
Pink 36
    Red 242
Chalcopyrite 241
Challenge ix, xi, xiii, xv, 42, 58, 65,
        251
Chakras xxiv, 23, 69, 105–11,
        112, 131, 142, 148, 152, 153,
        155, 175, 212, 213, 214, 218,
        220
    Base 106, 110, 111, 129, 150,
        152, 153, 214, 218
    Balancing creams 225
    Earth/root 7, 105, 110, 111,
        150, 213
    Heart 7, 107, 150, 151, 152,
        153, 155, 177, 212
    Heart Seed 223, 224, 225, 226
    Higher 9, 45, 223–7
    Higher Earth 224, 225, 226,
        227
    Higher Heart 107, 114, 150,
        151, 155, 157, 177, 212
        224, 225, 226

Lower 7, 155
Sacral 106, 111, 150, 152, 153, 175, 235
Solar plexus xx, 7, 17, 27, 101, 102, 107, 111, 119, 127, 129, 150, 151, 152, 175, 177, 215
Soma 108, 131, 132, 150, 153, 222, 224, 225, 226, 231
Soul Star 45, 109 224, 226,
Spleen 113, 117, 119, 121, 132, 133
Stellar Gateway 45, 109, 224
Change xi, xii, xiii, xv, xvi, xix, 24, 29, 31, 32, 33, 34, 41–3, 48, 57, 59, 60, 66, 72, 85, 107, 123, 135–41, 154, 155, 172, 174, 187, 195–7, 199, 205, 213–14, 223, 228, 233, 238, 244, 251
Charoite 100, **154**, 156
Chiastolite 156
Children 59, 102, 179, 199, 201, 247
Chiron 154
Chrysocolla **165**, 171
Cinnabar 241
Citrine 10, 49, 59, 156, 170, 171, 241, 245
Clear2Light 72, 77, 81, 83, 85, 191
Clear Tone 125,
Clingy relationships 47
Compassion xxviii, 54, 56, 107 120, 147, 148, 150, 160, 195, 224, 226
Compulsions 154
Confidence xv, xxi, xxvii, 19, 33, 34, 58, 59, 65, 106, 124, 144, 148, 150, 159, 171, 192, 215, 230
Confusion 41, 148
Cooperation 48, 93
Covellite 171, **209**, 210
Crinoidal Limestone **60**, 61

Crystal
Balance 81
Cleansing and charging 12–13
Cleanser 13, 72
Colours
Black xxiii
Brown 3, 7, 28
Green 7
Indigo 7
Lilac 7
Orange 7, 243
Pink 7, 222
Red 7, 78, 91, 243
Smoky 7
Yellow 7
White 7, 12, 19, 222
Egg 22
EFT 65–6, 130–41
Lattice xxiii, 14, 184
Programming 6, 12, 15, 33, 48, 78, 182, 183, 223, 234, 241, 242
Recharge 12–14, 146
Cuprite with Chrysocolla *see* Sonora Sunrise
Curse 85, 186, 190, 191, 254

D
Darwin, Charles xv
Dalmatian Stone 30, 153
Danburite 46, 91, 220, 223, 225
Depression xxiii, 84, 113, 169, 173–5, 182
Desert Rose 33
Detachment Spray 120, 121, 193
Detoxification 127, 151
Bath 128–9
Layout 127
Diamond 74, 101, 156, 241
Dioptase 144
Dis-ease 13, 18, 24, 25, 39, 61, 69, 70, 86, 101, 105, 112–15, 130, 157, 174, 216, 218
Dream Catcher 102
Dumortierite 46, 59, 156, 171
Dustbin 48, 169, 200

E

Earthlight 77
Eclipse Stone **228**
EFT 65, 65–6, 130–41
Egypt xxi, 96, 188
Electromagnetic stress xxvii, xxx, 7, 8, 50, 71, 73, 74, 86, 89, 92, 93, 94, 115, 122, 144, 184, 254
E-mail attack 198
Emerald **37**, 44, 241
Emergency 48, 76, 86, 97, 122, 124, 196
Emotional xxix, 7, 18, 25, 34, 51, 65, 73, 87, 101, 107, 112, 113, 148, 150, 157, 174, 189, 205, 210, 228
    baggage 41, 133, 158, 160, 210
    Balance/equilibrium 150, 152, 175
    Causes of dis-ease 18
    Cleansing/detox 73, 111, 127, 130, 173
    Conditioning 145, 165
    Connection/disconnection 107, 189
    Healing 135
    Hooks 103
    Independence 59
    Manipulation 102
    Recovery 74, 112
    Stress 142
    Transformation 7, 41
    Well-being 14
Energetic shield 47
Energy
    Block 48
    Bodies 223
    Boost xvii, xxi, 3, 24, 50, 59, 81, 131, 146, 205, 243
    Cleanse/transmute xxiv, 14, 41, 54, 71, 92, 110, 172, 182, 184, 190
    Core 62, 145, 206, 214, 215, 219
    Depletion/drain/loss xii, xxiv, xxix, 8, 98, 101, 107, 113, 117–21, 122, 182
    Earth xxiv, 9, 87, 226
    Field xx, 76, 120, 123, 224
    Focus 7
    Grids 89–92, 224
    Ground 216
    Imprint 75, 84, 197
    Noxious/negative/toxic x, xxiii, xxvii, xxix, 8, 9, 10, 13, 16, 23, 69, 73, 74, 83, 88, 98, 112, 131, 147, 163, 168, 176, 178, 184, 186, 207
    Pirates/vampires xxviii, 70, 93, 97, 98, 113, 117–21
    Positive 7, 15, 23, 24
    Protective/shield 6, 9, 21, 24, 25, 30, 33, 47–9
    Recharge/reprogramme 130, 131, 145–6, 153, 161
    Spiritual/divine/loving 153, 157, 177, 189, 210, 219, 221–2
    Stabilise 28
Environmental pollution xxvii, 10, 13, 26, 69, 71, 72, 83, 88, 92, 93, 113, 122, 214
Epidote 171, 213
Essences xxviii, 18–19, 72, 81–3, 85, 86, 93, 94, 98, 123, 125, 126, 129, 150, 170, 175, 191, and *see* individual essences
Etheric blueprint 218, 220
Exorcism 167
Eye of the Storm 153, 158, 166, 173, 175, 196, 208, 210

F

Family 71, 95, 102, 173
    Line 95
    Patterns 54
    Protect 62, 200–1
Fear xvi, xviii, xxv, xxvii, xxxiii, 3, 20, 24, 39, 41, 63, 71, 72, 106, 108, 112, 113, 130, 135, 136,

139–40, 147, 151, 152, 153–6,
162, 164, 170, 173, 175, 178,
179, 182, 183, 185, 193, 199,
206, 207, 213, 222
Fearless 138, 190
Feeling positive 228
Feldspar, Red 78
Figure of eight 89, **91**
Fire Opal 171
Flint 6, 11, 27, **28**, 30, 44, 46, 53,
76, 100, 101, 118, 121, 126,
171, 213
Fluorite 74, 144
Green 121
Food, energise 243
Forgiveness xxviii, 7, 57, 77, 95,
103, 120, 124, 125, 134, 147,
151, 157–8, 161, 178, 189,
190, 195, 198, 224
Fortune, Dion ix, xi, 176, 186
Fringed Violet 126
Fulgarite 44, 172

G
Galaxyite **207**
Garnet 172
Grossular **237**, 238, 241, 242
Gaspeite 121, 142
Gem essences xxviii, 18–19, 72,
81–6, 93, 94, 98, 123, 125, 126,
129, 150, 170, 171, 175, 91
Geopathic stress/geopathogens
xvii, xxvii, xxix, 7, 8, 13, 22,
50, 71, 73, 74, 84, 92, 94, 115
Ghosts xvii, xxviii, 197, 200
Goals 205, 233, 234, 242
Goldstone **237**, 241
Gratitude 32, 56, 57, 62, 95, 230,
245
Green Ridge Quartz **66**
Gridding xxiv, 8, 10, 13, 14, 15, 16,
34, 57, 58, 71, 73, 74, 77, 87
88, 89–92, 99, 122, 131, 153
170, 183, 191, 193, 224, 237
Grounding 8, 9, 10, 17, 26, 28,
29, 30, 46, 48, 53, 58, 91,

106, 111, 145, 146, 161, 184,
196, 206, 207, 213, 214, 218,
219, 222, 227
Guilt xxvii, xxx, 63, 113, 152

H
Halite 12, **14**, 56, 72, 127, 128,
171
Happiness 5, 9, 57, 59, 61, 184
Hematite xxi, 10, 27, 28, 30, 49,
59, **80**, 98, 129, 171
Heart xiii, xix, xxiii, xxiv, xxv, xxviii,
7, 8, 9, 17, 29, 41, 45, 54, 61,
97, 107, 111, 114, 119, 122,
127, 129, 133, 150, 151, 152,
153, 155, 158, 175, 177, 207,
208, 209, 212, 222, 223, 237,
240, 245
Higher chakra 224, 225
Points 134
Seed chakra 224, 225
Temple of 209–10
Herkimer Diamond 71, 74, 101
Hexagram 15, 52, 89, 192, 239,
240
Hidden parts/programmes xxvi, 32,
134, 154, 169, 174, 195
Howlite 44

I
Ill-wishing 8, 11, 13, 50, 62, 79,
92, 176, 178–84, 191, 194
Immune
Stimulator 92, 115–16, 129
system xvii, 25, 34, 70, 73,
105, 112–15, 117, 121,
129, 142, 144, 145, 147
Inner
smile 60–1
terrorist x, xxvii, xxxiii, 194–6
wealth 237
Intention xxiii, xxvii, 12, 17, 18,
30–3, 36, 37, 40, 47, 49,
55, 57, 65, 76, 78, 79, 81, 82,
86, 87, 98, 100, 124, 136, 141,
166, 183, 187, 201, 209, 251

Iolite 38
Iron Pyrite **33**, 44, 171, 216, 241

J
Jade **43**, 44, 101, 102, 121, 241
Jasper 6, 12, 16, **26**, 27, 74, 171
    Brown 30
    Bumble Bee **63**, 64
    Green 101
    Kambaba **26**, 30
    Judy's see Eye of the Storm
    Leopardskin 64, 156
    Ocean 166
    Polychrome 9, **184**, 189
    Poppy 129, **146**
    Red 30, 78, 91, 111, 127, 129,
       150, 165, **214**
    Yellow 17, 111, 127, 129,
       144, 150
Jet 156
Journeying xxii, 9, 16, 17, 26, 29,
    38, 39, 42, 47, 48, 50, 53–5,
    63–5, 192, 207, 209–10, 216,
    230–3
Juju 185

K
Karmic
    Astrology 230
    Blueprint 216
    readings 256
Keyiapo **216**
Kick-ass combination 77
Koolman, Margaret xiii, 248–9
Kunzite xxiii, 74, 91, 144, 171, 174
Kyanite 88, 242

L
Labradorite **xiii**, 8, 36, 38, 39,
    92, 93, 101, 121, 144, 156,
    174, 175, 191, 219
Language xvi, 42, 43, 251
    Body xx, 213–16
Larimar **63**, 64, 196, 245
Layouts 14–15, 17–18, 89–92,
    127, 174, 241

Lazulite 59, 171
Leadership 93
Lemurian Jade 101
Lepidolite 74, 144
Letting go 16, 31, 127, 128, 136,
    160, 171, 212
Lichen 126
Light xxii, 16, 77, 82, 86, 100,
    102, 110, 111, 119, 122, 125,
    136, 146, 160, 161, 168, 197,
    228, 237, 243
    Body 10, 45
    Bubble 20–2, 23, 46, 47, 48,
       70, 98, 120, 121, 124,
       160, 178, 189, 193, 196,
       206
    Divine/spiritual 8, 45, 92, 99,
       221, 224
    Golden 24, 170
    Moon 12, 96
    Pink 77, 134, 182,199, 200
    Psychic 163
    Sun 12, 14, 96, 241
    White 129, 146, 225
Life plan 230–5
Like attracts like 31, 87
Lodolite **54**, 55
Lost soul 122, 124–6, 167

M
Magnesite 44
Malachite 38, 88, 92, 241
Manifestation crystal see Quartz
Marcasite 49
Master Shamanite 189, **192**
Meditation 42, 43, 81, 112, 142,
    169, 217–21
Mental
    Causes of disease 18, 25
    Influence 163, 165
    Mirror 190
    Overload/stress 142, 144,
       162–4
    Pattern 147, 164, 165, 193
    Pollutants/baggage 66, 73,
       113, 133, 164

Positivity 206
Problems 21, 112, 157, 170,
    172–3
Program xviii, xxix, xxxiii, 13,
    145, 188
Merlinite 55, 171
Mid-life crisis 172
Mind's Eye 4, 23, 37, 38, 48, 76,
    119, 247
Moonstone 220
    Blue 242
Morganite 46, 245
Motivation 22, 145, 146, 170, 237
Multi-dimensions 9, 10, 16, 21,
    38, 48, 52, 55, 123, 218, 220,
    223, 225
Muscovite 46, 245

N
Negative x, xvi, xxv, 21, 39, 43,
    52, 76, 82, 84, 93, 130, 147,
    156, 176, 245
Emotions xxvi, xxix, 7, 65, 85, 103,
    105, 127–9, 130, 145, 147,
    150, 174, 175–6, 188, 200,
    209, 214, 228
Energy xxi, xxiii, xxiv, xxvii, xxix,
    8, 9, 10, 13, 15, 16, 21, 22,
    23, 47, 71, 73, 79, 82, 85, 86,
    88, 92, 94, 99, 112, 131, 184,
    206, 207, 214
Expectation 36, 162, 228,
Thoughts/belief 14, 20, 32, 39, 42,
    43, 65, 69, 112, 130, 154,
    162, 164, 178, 183, 188, 196,
    228
Neurosis 172
Novaculite 118, 121, 126
Nunderite 9, 18, 48, 49, 144
Nuummite 10, 49, 118, 126, 172,
    182

O
Obsidian 55
    Black 85

Mahogany 171
Rainbow 166, 172, 182, 198,
    221
Oil 81, 86, 128, 129
    burner 55
    Frankincense 79
Okenite 242
Onyx 171
Out of my space 75
Outworn ideas/emotion 32, 172

P
Panic attack 75, 172, 183
Peace xv, 7, 45, 54, 56, 57, 58,
    59, 60, 66, 93, 97, 99, 144,
    151, 157, 206–10, 213,
    216, 218, 228, 238
Pearl Spa Dolomite 153
Peridot **192**, 241, 245, 246
Pelvis 214, 215–6
Pentacle 89
Pentagram 15, 50–1, 52, 70, 89,
    90–1
Petaltone 72, 77, 81, 82, 125,
    126, 177, 225
Phenacite 78, **218**, 220
Pietersite 210
Porphyrite **35**
Positive thought 42–4, 57, 197
Prana 105
Prehnite 38, 213
Preseli Bluestone 9, 30, **38**, 54, 55,
    171, 226
Present moment xxxiii, 40, 55,
    155, 205, 234, 248–9
Prosperity 8, 15, 16, 93, 122
Psychiatric conditions 163, 172,
    176
Psychic
    Abilities 8
    Attack ix, x, xvii, xxviii, 13, 21,
        48, 112, 176–99
    Immune system 25, 70, 105,
        112–15, 147
    Leakage 97

Mugging x, xvii, xxiv, xxviii, 8,
   112, 176–8, 189, 194,
   200, 201
Protection ix, xi, xii, xvi, xix–xxi,
   xxx, xxxi–ii, 23, 34, 44, 62,
   70, 83, 144, 186, 200
Residue 84
Safety 251
Shields 47–9
Shock 112
Vampires xxxiii, 13, 98,
   117–22, 142
Pumice 172
Purpurite 49, 59, 171
Pyramid: xxxii, 169, 201
   Golden 23, 24, 72, 86
   Green 117, 119, 121

Q
Quantum Quattro 71, 74, 114,
   116, 129, 144, 153, 170
Quartz
   Amphibole 46, 82, 83, 91
   Apple Aura 121
   Aqua Aura 101
   Candle 46, 59, 124, 125, 126,
      156, 241
   Cathedral 230
   Chlorite 49, 88, 92
   Elestial **41**, 42, 46, 55, 74, 86,
      89, 96, 177, 225, 226, 245
      Smoky **16**, 30
   Fenster 171
   Fire and Ice **220**, 221
   Golden **25**
   Green Ridge 38, 55, **66**, 101,
      102, 144, 153, 159, 177,
      223, 235, 245
   Laser xxii, 110, 118, 119, 121,
      125, 173
   Lavender 245
   Lemurian Seed 10, 46, 110,
      121, 131, 159, 177, 220
   Manifestation 241
   Milk 6, 11, 53
   Nirvana 213, 220, 223, 226

Phantom 33, 38, 46, 54, 55,
   171, 230
Pink Crackle **59**, 61, 166, 172
Rose **7**, 8, 17, 33, 36, 41, 42,
   57, 61, 89, 116, 118, 126,
   129, 142, 144, 149, 150,
   151, 157, 158, 166, 171,
   172, 174, 177, 196, 210,
   222, 225, 245
Rutilated (Angel's Hair) **24**, 46,
   171, 172, 196
Shaman **54**, 55
Smoky xxiii, 8, 10, **16**, 17, 18,
   28, 30, 49, 65, 71, 74, 78,
   88, 89, 91, 94, 101, 110,
   115, 127, 150, 151, 166,
   173, 174, 175, 177, 182,
   217, 220, 226
Snow see Milk
Spirit 55, 91, 93, 94, 95, 126,
   173, 213, 245
Strawberry 59, 171
Tibetan Black Spot 159
Tourmalinated 88, 196
Trigonic 213
Que Sera 114, **115**, 116

R
Rainbow Mayanite 9, 101, 118,
   123, 125, 126, 213
Red Feldspar with Phenacite 78
Reframing 14, 40, 42, 43, 165
Rejection 14
Relaxation 17, 18, 92, 128, 129,
   142, 229, 238
Release 9, 15, 39, 47, 56, 65, 85,
   118, 120, 122, 123, 125, 127,
   133, 135, 144, 149, 152, 153,
   160, 164, 165, 166, 173, 175,
   178, 193, 209, 215
Responsibility 103, 164
Revisioning 159
Rhodochrosite **56**, 57, 171, 177, 210
Rhyolite 59
Richterite 9, **43**, 144
Root 29–30, 53, 55, 60, 156, 218

Of fears 154
Of problem 24, 54
Rosophia **155**, 157
Ruby 44, 241
Rutherford, Leo 69
Rutile 24, 55, 186

S
Sacred xii, 228
  geometry 49
  site 21, 84, 95–6
  space 23, 40–1
  symbols 23
Safe space xii, xix, xxiv, xxv, xxxii,
  23, 50, 70, 71–4, 75, 86–92,
  150, 159, 169, 192, 206
Sage 55, 79, 86
Salt 12, 50, 127, 128, 129, 177
Sapphire 36, 210, 241
Sardonyx 87, 88, 92
Scapolite 196, **234**
Scars 97
Seasonal affective disorder 164
Selenite 8, 12, 38, 42, 46, 77, 82,
  83, 88, 89, 91, 92, 96, **99**, 100,
  101 111, 191, 210, 213, 220,
  222
Self-esteem 58, 106, 113, 150,
  171, 228
Self-expression 58
Self-sabotage 196, 234
Self, manifest 211–13
Serenity xxxii, 18, 43, 54, 63, 87,
  97, 147, 157, 209–10, 215,
  248, 249
Serpentine 64, 95, 213
Shattuckite with Ajoite 101
Shungite 9, 49, 71, **73**, 74, 88, 89,
  92, 94, 116, 144, 182, 183, 189
Sick building syndrome xvii, 94
Slender Rice Flower 98
Smithsonite **34**, 36, 92, 116, 129
Smudging 55–6, 77, 79, 86, 96,
  191
Sodalite 36, 59, 94, 111, 116,
  127, 150, 172, 173, 220

Solomon's Seal 52
Sonora Sunrise **165**
Soul(s) xix, 28, 35, 54, 57, 60, 85,
  109, 122, 155, 216, 222, 243,
  244, 248, 249
  Gifts 228, 230
  healer 218
  imperatives 10
  lost/stuck 81, 122, 123, 124–6,
    167
  plan/path/purpose 62, 207, 211,
    224, 226, 230, 233, 242
  Shield 77, 81, 129
Sound 79, 96
Space
  Clearing/cleansing tools xii, 24,
    55–6, 71–4, 75–7, 77,
    79–80, 170
  Crystals 86–92
  Essences 81–6
  invasion 74–5, 89
  sacred 41–2, 49, 95–7
  safe xix, xxiv, xxv, xxx, xxxii, 23,
    40, 43, 55, 70, 71–4, 95,
    150, 159, 169, 192, 206
Spacesuit 201
Special 8 77, 81, 82, 124, 126
Spiral 15, 100, 133
Spirit, calling home 65–6
Spirits, stuck 76, 81, 82, 122–6
Spleen point 113, 117, 119, 121,
  133
Square 15, 33
Stagnant energy 54, 172
Star Hollandite 171
Star of David 52
Stibnite **47**, 49, 65
Stress 9, 16, 22, 25, 34, 42,
  43, 59, 113, 115, 142–4,
  146, 151, 154, 182, 184, 192,
  207, 214, 237
  Geopathic, EMF xvii, xxix, 7, 8,
    50, 71, 73, 74, 84, 92, 94,
    122
  Mental 173
Stromatolite **26**, 30

Strombolite 245
Sulphur 56
Sunstone **164**, 170, 175
Super 7 88, 91, 92, 126, 194, 196

T
Tantalite 9, **13**, 183, 189, 192
Tanzanite 46, 171, 211, 213
Tapping points 65, 132–5
Telephone 94
Temple of the heart 209
Thought control 154
Thymus 107, 114, 115, 116, 121, 127, 184, 189
Ti Essence 85, 191
Tiger's Eye 241, 242
Timeline 233, 234
Topaz 33, 170, 241, 242
Tourmaline xxiii
    Black 8, 10, 49, 71, 73, 74, 86, 88, 89, 92, 101, 121, 182, 183, **184**, 188, 189, 191, 192
    Dravide (Brown) 30
    Green 9, 101
    Paraiba 46, 172
    Watermelon 33
Toxic/negative emotions xvi, xviii, xxvi, xxxiii, 7, 21, 65, 71, 85, 103, 105, 113, 127–9, 130–141, 147–50, 151, 157, 158–61, 173, 175, 188, 200, 209
Tremolite 36, **58**, 59
Trust xvi, xvii, xviii, xxxiii, 31, 34–6, 46, 58, 62, 63, 94, 114, 140, 145, 147, 165, 167, 233, 237, 241

Tugtupite xxv, 36, 46, 57, 61, 121, 156, 177, 223, 225
Tumbled crystals 6, 7, 12, 22, 27
Turquoise 89, 196

U
Unconditional love 7, 8, 56, 77, 107, 109, 120, 134, 150, 153, 157, 158, 175, 178, 191, 222, 224, 226

V
Variscite **114**
Victim mentality 113, 164
Violet Flame 102
Vision boards 49, 102, 120, 208
Visioning xxxii, 20, 29, 37–40, 42, 53, 95, 120–1, 158–61, 194, 201, 234

W
Wisdom 37, 39, 62, 212, 232
Workspace 71, 85, 93–4
Worry xvi, xviii, xxv, xxxi, 16, 31, 36, 59, 74, 131, 147, 165–7, 172, 248, 251
    pot 166
Wounds, heal 154

Z
Z14 81, 82, 83, 118, 125, 126, 187, 191, 197
Zebra stone 171
Zincite 242
Zoisite 211, 213

ABOUT THE AUTHOR

Judy Hall is an internationally recognized author, crystal expert, astrologer, psychic, healer, broadcaster and workshop leader. She has a BEd in Religious Studies and a Masters Degree in Cultural Astronomy and Astrology, and has an extensive knowledge of world religions and mythology. Her numerous books have been translated into 18 languages.

www.judyhall.co.uk and
www.angeladditions.co.uk

Made in the USA
San Bernardino, CA
30 June 2014